Praise for *The Plum Tree Blossoms Even in Winter*

"M. Roy Wilson's memoir of overcoming personal, family, and social challenges to become a leader in higher education and in the health professions is truly inspiring. His courage, persistence, and high standards for achievement, integrity, and service show the heights one can reach with determination and focus. Many individuals and institutions are the beneficiaries of his successful journey."

—Louis W. Sullivan, U.S. Secretary of Health and Human Services, 1989–1993 and President Emeritus, Morehouse School of Medicine

"*The Plum Tree Blossoms Even in Winter* shines brightest when it illuminates Dr. Wilson's unwavering dedication to caring for marginalized patients, serving underserved populations, giving voice to the voiceless, and creating pathways forward for those who may not have seen that pathway for themselves. The long arc of his career has lifted and empowered the lives of thousands of patients, students, and medical professionals in classrooms and clinics around the world. In the end, one is left with an uplifting story of the joy and privilege of service. This is a wonderful message for all during these trying times."

—Michael V. Drake, President, University of California

"A powerful and poignant autobiography by M. Roy Wilson. The reader is immersed into the opportunities and challenges of being born Black and Asian; it is relevant in today's global perspectives on race and equality. Important life lessons are derived from a challenging upbringing that included discrimination and abandonment. Personal strength is derived from the traditions of Japanese and Black culture. These lessons served Dr. Wilson well as he ascended into the presidency of several universities and medical schools. We can all learn from this remarkable life story."

—Francisco Cigarroa, Chair, Board of Trustees, Ford Foundation and former Chancellor of the University of Texas System

"An intriguing window into a life well lived! M. Roy Wilson generously shares the wisdom earned through [his] many struggles with a sense of introspection and insight that is inspiring."

—Anne L. Coleman, Fran and Ray Stark Professor of Ophthalmology, David Geffen School of Medicine, UCLA and past President of the American Academy of Ophthalmology

"*The Plum Tree Blossoms Even in Winter* reminds me that we are all unique, each with our own challenges and opportunities that we must face or seize, depending on our abilities, resolve, and tenacity. Throughout his extraordinary life, M. Roy Wilson contended with hardships and trials that would break the spirit of most people, let alone a young boy on his own and far from home. In each case he persevered, he overcame, he adapted, and he learned. His dogged determination and indefatigable work ethic propelled him from the streets to the highest levels of medicine, research, and higher education. This book is a gripping read and an inspiration for anyone who faces obstacles on the way to achieving their dreams and becoming their best selves."

—Allan Gilmour, eleventh President of Wayne State University and former Vice-Chairman of Ford Motor Company

"*I resolved to always look to the future and continue to develop and evolve— throughout life.*' We are fortunate to witness M. Roy Wilson's resolve and forward vision as he makes a difference every day in Detroit and in Michigan. His courage in sharing his story is a small example of his lifelong commitment to ensuring that education and learning are accessible to and valued by all."

—Cindy Pasky, CEO, Strategic Staffing Solutions

"M. Roy Wilson's captivating and engaging memoir tells the story of remarkable and unprecedented achievements through overcoming incredible and heartrending adversity. Every page is a life lesson that no matter the odds, with courage, faith, and perseverance one can become a great role model, as M. Roy Wilson has become for me and so many others."

—Gary Torgow, Chairman, Huntington Bank

"*The Plum Tree Blossoms Even in Winter* reveals the fascinating life journey of an extraordinary man. Through the prism of this sincerely honest and thoughtfully reflective autobiography, M. Roy Wilson offers a complex narrative that is nevertheless refreshingly simple in its fidelity to the author's deeply principled humanity. The lived experience of this biracial, athletically talented physician who was raised in both Japan and the United States paints a compelling portrait of perseverance through a life of challenges that produced one of this nation's most important academic and physician leaders. The audience for this book is, like its author, diverse, but this memoir will be of special interest to all students who are navigating the contours of their own life journeys."

—Reed Tuckson, former President of the Charles Drew University of Medicine and Science and former Executive Vice President and Chief of Medical Affairs for United Health Group

THE
PLUM TREE
BLOSSOMS
EVEN IN
WINTER

THE
PLUM TREE
BLOSSOMS
EVEN IN
WINTER

M. ROY WILSON

WAYNE STATE UNIVERSITY PRESS
Detroit

ISBN 978-0-8143-4980-9 (jacketed cloth)
ISBN 978-0-8143-4979-3 (paperback)
ISBN 978-0-8143-4981-6 (e-book)

Library of Congress Control Number: 2022930697

Cover photo by Jacqueline Page Productions. Cover design by Brad Norr Design.

All of the names mentioned in this memoir are accurate to the best of my memory. Some names have been altered to protect the identity of certain parties.

Wayne State University Press rests on Waawiyaataanong, also referred to as Detroit, the ancestral and contemporary homeland of the Three Fires Confederacy. These sovereign lands were granted by the Ojibwe, Odawa, Potawatomi, and Wyandot nations, in 1807, through the Treaty of Detroit. Wayne State University Press affirms Indigenous sovereignty and honors all tribes with a connection to Detroit. With our Native neighbors, the press works to advance educational equity and promote a better future for the earth and all people.

Wayne State University Press
Leonard N. Simons Building
4809 Woodward Avenue
Detroit, Michigan 48201-1309

Visit us online at wsupress.wayne.edu.

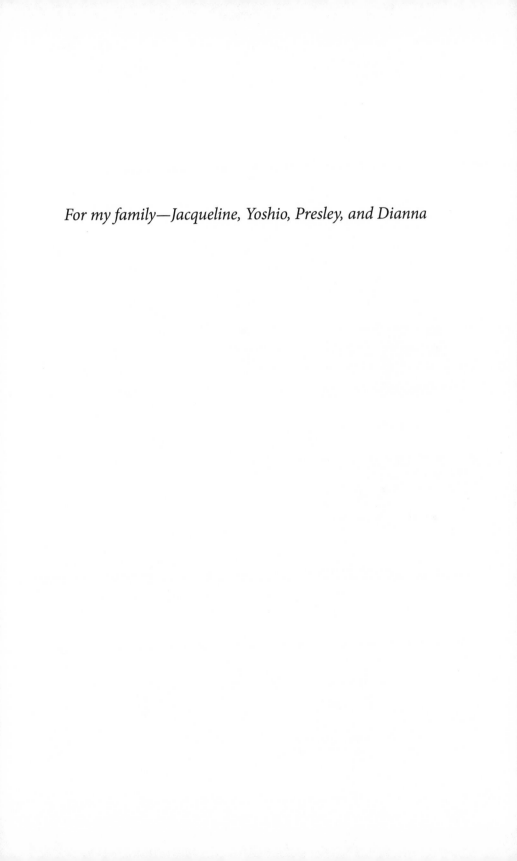

For my family—Jacqueline, Yoshio, Presley, and Dianna

Contents

Prologue

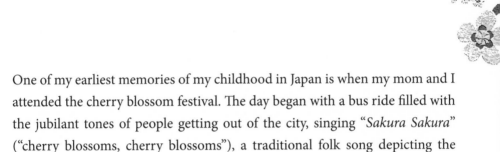

One of my earliest memories of my childhood in Japan is when my mom and I attended the cherry blossom festival. The day began with a bus ride filled with the jubilant tones of people getting out of the city, singing *"Sakura Sakura"* ("cherry blossoms, cherry blossoms"), a traditional folk song depicting the spring.

On the way home from the festival, we stopped at a Shinto temple where my mom wanted to pray. My mom was a Buddhist but that didn't matter. Like many Japanese, she observed both Shinto and Buddhism and didn't see any conflict or contradiction between the two.

Afterward, we stopped in a little store that sold snacks and souvenir ornaments. An etching of flower blossoms caught my eye. Wanting to remember the day, I asked my mom to purchase it for me.

When we returned home, I asked her to read the inscription next to the image. I was profoundly disappointed when she read, "The Plum Tree Blossoms Even in Winter." I thought it was an etching of cherry blossoms, not plum blossoms!

Nevertheless, I came to treasure that memento from my childhood, perhaps because its meaning was even more profound than I could have understood at the time. My mom raised me by herself for the first years of my life, so we were very close. A few years later, she became addicted to gambling and I rarely saw her. I was often alone, without parental guidance or affection, and

I yearned for those earlier times when my mom and I were together, as on that cherry blossom trip. I kept that memento until I placed it in Mom's casket.

The anticipation of spring is implicit in the popular rhyme "April showers bring May flowers." The flowers of most trees, including the cherry tree, bloom in the spring. The plum tree is special in that it blooms early, often in February, the coldest, dreariest month of the year. To many, as it is to me, it's a symbol of resilience and perseverance.

It would be difficult to imagine a better symbol of my life. My childhood was a time of loneliness and deprivation. And as an adult, I encountered health challenges for which the expected outcome was blindness in one case and death in the other. Through it all, I never despaired. Through it all, I persevered. The plum tree serves as a reminder that out of darkness and bleakness can emerge hope, strength, transcendent beauty.

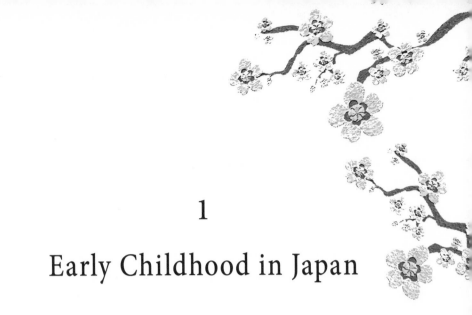

1

Early Childhood in Japan

Many Americans regard the Eisenhower years as an idyllic time. Following the privations of World War II, this was a period of national prosperity, when the men who had served in the armed forces were able to attain an education, a good income, and homeownership. But what of the men who were still overseas?

My dad, James O. Wilson Jr., grew up in Youngstown, Ohio, in a large Black family that included nine siblings. Practically everyone in his neighborhood worked in the steel mills. After graduating from high school, my father enlisted in the Navy. Shortly afterward, on June 25, 1950, North Korea invaded South Korea and in a matter of days, U.S. land, air, and sea forces had joined the battle in support of South Korea. My dad was among those deployed there before being stationed at the naval base in Yokohama, Japan, where he met my mother.

My mom, Katsu Katsuumi, had grown up with relatives in a rural town in the Gunma Prefecture and left as soon as she was old enough to support herself. Fleeing poverty and abuse, she moved to the Yokohama area. She was working as a waitress at a local restaurant near the naval base when she met my father in 1952. I don't know the details of their early relationship. Because she worked at a restaurant that catered mainly to military personnel, my mom at least understood some rudimentary English. I like to imagine my parents' first conversations.

I was born at a hospital in Yokohama on Saturday, November 28, 1953, three years after the bloody and frustrating Korean War had commenced, and several months after the armistice was signed, suspending open hostilities. It is estimated that by 1952, anywhere from five thousand to ten thousand children were born to Japanese women and American servicemen. Many of the children born from these unions were placed for adoption due to both the stigma of being born out of wedlock and miscegenation taboos. Those who were mixed race with Black fathers were frequently abandoned. I wonder if my mom, at age twenty-four, felt ashamed at having me out of wedlock, if she considered putting me up for adoption, or, worse, if she considered abandoning me. I wonder also if my dad thought about abandoning her and their child. Or perhaps he reassured her of his good intentions and she believed that my having an American father would provide security.

I know a few details about my birth. My mom was a small woman, and she often recounted how difficult her pregnancy was because I was so big (I was a ten-pound baby). It was a difficult birth. At one point, the doctor attempted a forceps delivery, from which I still have marks near my temple, but a Caesarean section was ultimately necessary.

Whatever his intentions, my dad was not around after my birth. They had not yet married, and it must have been a very difficult time for my mom. She often told the story of how adorable I was as a baby and how someone offered to pay a huge sum of money to buy me. She refused and took care of me as best as she could, carrying me on her back as she worked at whatever job she could find and clothing me in paper when she couldn't afford fabric.

I am not clear on the timing, but Dad started visiting us when we lived outside Yokohama, but I have no recollection of these visits. However, I do have vague but fond memories of an older man with white hair and a stooped back whom I referred to as Ojiisan.

In Japanese, the terms for "grandpa" and "uncle" differ by only a single character, an additional "i." I know that this older man was neither, because my mom's father and brother both died during the war. Mom didn't discuss the circumstances of their deaths with me, but the last time she saw them was when they left her to join the Japanese war effort against the United States. I recall that the older man I called Ojiisan was nice, and although he was small and visibly hunched, he would sometimes carry me on his back. As I now think back to this time, I realize that my mom had to financially support the two of us, and that Ojiisan likely volunteered or was hired to look after me when she couldn't take me to work.

My mom was a gambler. She once told me the story of how she got mired in it. Initially she gambled not so much to win money but out of boredom and curiosity. After she won a huge sum during one of her first games, she and my dad had a fight about it that became physical; she ended up hitting Dad and he kicked her in the stomach in self-defense. Upset, she blew through the money, giving most of it away. Later, she regretted what she had done, and she gambled more to try to win it back. Sometimes she did win, but despite her obsession, Mom was never able to re-create that first high.

I would sometimes accompany her to the gambling house, where she would play *cho-han*, a dice game, with an almost exclusively male group. Japan's organized crime syndicate, the Yakuza, controlled cho-han gambling so I was often in their company. The Yakuza spoke with a distinct guttural tone. Gruff and intimidating, the men were often shirtless, displaying their elaborate body tattoos. They walked with a swagger, their gait duck-footed and arms swinging more excessively than necessary, while I sat in the corner reading and rereading whatever beginner English books my mom could find for me to pass the time—folktales like "Three Little Pigs" and "Little Red Riding Hood." I don't recall receiving formal instruction in reading or speaking English, but perhaps my dad taught me the basics during his occasional visits. For the most part the Yakuza tolerated my presence and just ignored me. I didn't think then that they were at all bad, but it strikes me now that they were—as was my mother's lifelong addiction to gambling, an addiction that would take a tremendous toll on her children.

Mom sometimes gambled at night, but usually we went to the gambling house during the day. I preferred the day because I was allowed to take a break from reading and go to the Japanese water garden outside the gambling house.

There was a large koi pond spanned by a wooden walking bridge, where I would sit and look out at the beautiful scenery. Koi are Japanese carp, bred beginning in the nineteenth century in Niigata, Japan. I didn't know it then but koi is the national fish of Japan. I would stare at the majestic fish, whose spectacular coloration transported me out of the cacophony of the gambling room and into a world of tranquility and wonderment. My favorite koi was a big white one with a solitary, round, red spot on its head.

I don't know where my dad had been stationed, but when I was not quite five years old, he returned to live with us permanently, and Mom and Dad got married. By then, he had switched from the Navy to the Air Force and was stationed at Johnson Air Base in Sayama. To be with him, we moved from Yokohama to the city of Sayama, Saitama Prefecture, about nineteen miles northwest of Tokyo, where my sister, Dianna, was born on July 21, 1958. I remember the smile on my dad's face as he held my little sister in his arms. I don't recall how I felt about Dianna's arrival, but I resented Dad's presence in my life. I perceived him as gruff and mean and very unlike the Ojiisan who carried me on his back.

My childhood up to this time had been as a Japanese and with just my mom, so the move to Sayama to be with my dad was traumatic. In Yokohama, my favorite food had been onigiri (Japanese rice balls) stuffed with salted salmon and wrapped with seaweed. I had loved having that for lunch, particularly when the onigiri was grilled. Breakfast had typically been misoshiru (miso soup). But my dad demanded that I be Americanized. With the move to Sayama came Cheerios for breakfast and hamburgers and hot dogs for lunch. Moreover, I had left my Japanese friends in Yokohama and was expected to make friends with the American kids on base. Although I understood English, I was fluent in Japanese and much more comfortable interacting with Japanese kids.

I don't remember much about my dad during this time, but based on my later interactions with him, I think it's safe to assume that he was not warm and affectionate. At the same time, he probably wasn't the ogre I made him out to be. Whatever the reality, I rebelled and he didn't know how to handle it. I refused to speak English, didn't make American friends, and demanded

Japanese food. My guess is that we fed off each other's negativity until an endless feedback loop of antagonism was established.

Curiously, when my dad disciplined me, he allowed me to choose my punishment—either a spanking or isolation in a locked bathroom. Since I had never been spanked, I initially chose the isolation. But after I escaped through the narrow window above the toilet and ran off, that option was removed. My first spanking with a belt left welts on my backside and legs. I didn't want to go through that again and started to preemptively run away whenever I did anything that I thought might warrant punishment. Initially, I ran away to avoid a spanking; after a while I ran away because I just wanted to avoid my dad.

When I ran away, I would often stay gone for days at a time. At first, I didn't go far. After aimlessly walking the streets, I would sneak back into an alley on the bathroom side of the house and listen for voices. If the coast was clear, I would climb back into the house through the window and grab some food and extra clothing before climbing back out again. My parents eventually figured out what I was doing and bolted the window shut.

With the option of sneaking back into the house closed off, I ventured further into town and found ways to survive. Sayama was a small military town with a population of less than thirty-three thousand in 1960. We lived off base, just outside a barrier fence, in a house built by the American military. All the houses looked the same, single story and painted in similar shades of off-white. Most of our neighbors were military families, but I don't recall knowing any of them.

Business storage sheds were good places to take shelter. Sheds of restaurants were particularly good because I could also scavenge for food from their discarded garbage. Innovation and creativity were essential. Once I kicked a dog out of his rather nice and large doghouse and slept there.

Because I never planned to run away, whatever clothes I was wearing had to suffice. On one particularly cold winter night, without hat, coat, or gloves, the ground dusted with a light snow and icicles hanging from tree branches, I realized that my survival was dependent on finding shelter and warmth. I had turned down a side street and it was dark. Aside from the sound of the wind whistling and the occasional barking of a distant dog, it was quiet. My heart raced as I realized my ears and feet were beginning to freeze.

I started jogging, mainly to keep warm, and came upon a row of houses. I went to the first house and asked to be taken in for the night. After being refused, I moved on to the next house with similar results. The situation was getting dire when I finally came upon a house that allowed me in.

The couple was Japanese and they must have pitied me as I was likely shivering from the cold. The miso soup they fed me was the best I had ever tasted. The last thing I remember as I went to sleep was the warmth of the stove and blanket.

When I awoke the next morning, the police were in the house and arrested me. The couple who had provided me food and shelter knew my mom and had turned me in. Mom looked embarrassed as she tried to explain to the police how a young kid could have run away from home for so long without them being notified.

The experience of avoiding frostbite, and perhaps even a fate more grim, haunted me for years to come in the form of a recurring dream. In it, I was chased by a white, snowy figure covered in icicles. As I struggled to move my legs faster, the shadowy figure would get closer and closer before I would suddenly awaken. I was well into grade school before these dreams ceased.

More practically, the incident taught me a lesson: I had to venture further if I was going to run away. Not knowing who in town might know my mother, I began to take the local train to neighboring towns. Traveling on trains is easy in Japan. I spoke the language fluently and had a rudimentary understanding of the Japanese signs at the train station. As long as I had enough money to buy a ticket, it was not a problem.

Despite my dad's efforts to Americanize me, most of my friends were Japanese kids from an adjacent Japanese neighborhood. One of the things we did for fun was put rocks on railroad tracks, hide behind some shelter, and watch the rocks splinter into flying projectiles as the train ran over them. One day, the train conductor must have seen the rocks and, not wanting to risk riding over them, decided to stop. The train sounded a loud shriek as the brakes were applied, and the train chugged to a stop directly in front of our hiding place. We all ran, but my friends were older and ran faster. I couldn't get away fast enough and was caught by someone from the train and hauled to the police station.

When the police officers tried to coerce me into revealing the identity of my compatriots, I refused. They had stood by me during my ordeals with my dad, and I was not going to give them up. No charges were filed against me, probably because I was just a kid, but my mom's picture was in the newspaper the following day with a caption stating that her son had tried to derail a train. Of course, I hadn't been trying to derail a train. I was a confused kid desperately seeking a sense of belonging. I just wanted to be a part of the gang.

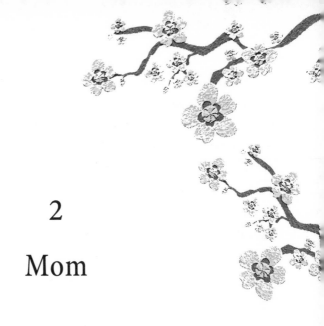

2

Mom

As did many Japanese of her generation, Mom had a difficult childhood. She didn't talk about it much. The Great Depression, which hit Japan especially hard, began in 1929, the year she was born. I've gleaned only snippets of her life during the pre–World War II years. She had two siblings, an older brother and a sister who died at a young age. My mom described her sister as having been beautiful, with very fair skin—a desirable trait among Japanese girls and women—but with a skeletal deformity. Her sister was frail and had difficulty breathing. In retrospect, I believe Mom was describing severe scoliosis (sideways curvature of the spine) with lung dysfunction as a result of reduced chest space.

My mom spoke lovingly of her older brother. She once said, "He took care of us," which I assumed to mean he took care of her and her sister. Because of her sister's frailty, her brother would often pick her up and carry her wherever she wanted to go. He was killed early in World War II, during a battle in the Pacific.

Mom rarely mentioned her father; when she did, it was usually just a matter-of-fact statement about him dying during the war. She didn't disclose enough for me to ascertain anything about him—what type of father he was, how she felt about him, what type of work he performed. I wish now that I had asked her more questions about the type of man he was and how he had died.

Since my mom never mentioned her mother, I always assumed she had died in the war, like her father and brother. As I think about it now, it was strange that she never mentioned her mother; it was almost as if she was not a part of her childhood. Over time, I became curious about who she had been and one day, when I was in high school, I asked Mom about her. What she told me came as a surprise. Her mother was a very accomplished—she may have even used the word "famous"—doctor in Tokyo. Since university education was available to only the elite in prewar Japan, and medical education for women was almost unheard of, my grandmother was indeed a trailblazer. I wondered if my grandmother was still alive, but Mom didn't know. They had lost touch with each other many years prior.

From what I could gather, my mom's early childhood was relatively uneventful. Then World War II happened and her life was indelibly impacted. With her mother busy pursuing her career and her father engaged in the war effort, my mom was left to the care of relatives in rural Gunma-ken, about seventy-five miles outside of Tokyo. When she was about twelve or thirteen, her mother brought her to live in Tokyo. But it was not a happy union (or reunion). Mom was often left alone while her mother worked. She mentioned "bombings," which was possibly a reference to the Doolittle Raid on Tokyo in April 1942. In any case, my mom must have been lonely and the bombing must have been a terrifying experience.

One day, when her mother was at work, Mom snuck out of school and caught a train back to Gunma-ken. Her mother came looking for her, but my mom refused to return. She felt more comfortable living a simple life with her paternal uncle and his family, even if it was a hard existence with few comforts. That was the last time they saw each other.

My mom didn't blame her mother or herself for their separate lives. She understood that her mother had to do what she did for her career. Likewise, she never expressed regret at leaving the city and returning to her comfort zone. Nor did she express embarrassment at being a country girl overwhelmed with the complexities of a big city. Rather, she seemed resigned to the fact that she and her mother were two different people who chose two different paths.

Later, her daughter, Dianna, would choose her own path at about the same age Mom had been when she decided to not live with her mother. Perhaps this is why Mom supported Dianna in her decision to leave home when she was just thirteen years old, when most parents would have reacted differently.

Life with her uncle, though preferable, was not idyllic. Her uncle was poor and he had his own family to feed: a wife and two kids who were not kind to their cousin. While his children attended school, my mom had to drop out of eighth grade to help her uncle on his farm. Her skin became parched from the sun and her hands blistered from the hard work. Rice and some pickled vegetables—no meat—made up her evening meal. In the morning, she would pour ocha—hot green tea—over days-old rice to soften it for breakfast.

On the heels of the Great Depression not having a lot to eat was understandable. But it was not simply a matter of being poor; my mom felt that her uncle's family mistreated her. Mom resented their treatment of her, partly because she was absolutely sure that her mother sent money every month to assist with expenses. Many years later, when she was a parent, no one would claim that she was good at it. However, perhaps because of her own experience growing up, she always made sure my sister and I had money, food, and clothes. And in her own limited way, she tried to show us that she loved us.

On my first visit home from medical school, my mom took my hand—such physical interaction was exceedingly rare—and looked me in the eye. She always used the honorific prefix of "san" rather than the more intimate "chan" when speaking to me. "Roy-san," she whispered, "my mother was a very good doctor. You will also be a good doctor. I'm so sorry you two never met." I have often been curious about my grandmother and would have liked to know more about her, but my mom never mentioned her again and I never asked.

When I was about six years old, Mom took my sister, Dianna, and me to visit her uncle and his wife in Gunma-ken. My mom beamed when she saw them and gave each a big hug. It was the only time I've ever seen her display public affection. As is the custom, all of us went to the sento (public bathhouse) during this visit, a large room with a tall barrier separating the sexes. It is customary to take baths at night, to wash away not only the sweat and dirt from the day but also the fatigue from a long day of work. In addition to a towel, a small bar of soap is often provided. In these bathhouses, the protocol is for people to wash themselves at stations equipped with a faucet for hot and cold water and a small wooden stool to sit on. After the body is thoroughly cleaned and rinsed, people soak in large communal tubs of different temperature levels lined up in a row.

My uncle and his wife would typically use that little bar of soap to wash everything, including their hair. This time, however, my mom bought each of them shampoo to wash their hair. They beamed and chatted excitedly like little kids; it was as if they had never used shampoo before. Mom depended on Dad for income so she didn't have much money, but as a military wife, the cost of a small single-use tube of shampoo would have been insignificant for her.

I never asked my mom why she had been so happy to see people who had treated her so badly. Perhaps she rationalized their bad behavior and forgave them. Or perhaps she had come to realize that life in postwar Japan was difficult and that circumstances for her would have been much worse had they not taken her in. This was the first time she had seen her aunt and uncle since she left to go to Yokohama, and I believe that she genuinely wanted to thank them as she left the past behind and embarked on her new life with her own family.

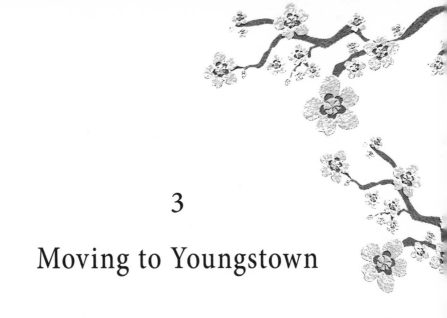

3

Moving to Youngstown

I had to repeat first grade in Japan because although I understood English, I refused to use it. I was also absent a lot, spending most of my days watching samurai movies on television and playing with my Japanese friends. Otherwise, I was running away from home and just surviving.

I became interested in the science of Freudian psychoanalysis in high school and once saw a psychoanalyst as a patient. At one of our early sessions, he remarked that my frequent running away from home seemed like a "rejection of Westernization." Actually, I had used that phrase earlier in discussing with him one of my favorite novels, *The Sea of Fertility*, Yukio Mishima's four-volume epic on Japanese life in the twentieth century. Mishima was a nationalist who extolled the traditional culture and spirit of Japan. Unsuccessful in thwarting the Westernization of Japan, he committed seppuku, the Japanese ritual suicide, after delivering the last installment of his manuscript to his publisher. Mishima ardently supported the immutable cultural unity of the Japanese, and in his rejection of Westernization, he made the ultimate sacrifice.

I don't know if the psychoanalyst's comment about rejecting Westernization had any validity or not. But I do know that I was very proudly Japanese at the time. I particularly loved the aspects of Japanese culture influenced by the samurais and their code of Bushido, with its eight virtues: rectitude or justice, courage, benevolence or mercy, politeness, honesty and sincerity, honor, loyalty, and character and self-control. Of these, I most admired the samurais' fidelity to honor and loyalty and believed these virtues best exemplified their persona.

Growing up, I watched a lot of samurai movies. I particularly liked Toshiro Mifune, who is known for his samurai roles in over 150 films—including *Rashomon* and *Seven Samurai*, as well as the NBC television miniseries *Shogun*. He is best remembered for his coarse, gruff voice, reminiscent of the Yakuza archetype. Later, as a young adult, I admired his performances so much that I convinced one of my mixed-race friends, Shinzato, to name his son, my god-son, Toshiro after him.

Although the samurai are often regarded as crude and ruthless, there is no denying that certain positive samurai concepts, codes, and ideals have permeated Japanese society and my life as well: the pursuit of excellence; the importance of honor, of principle; the idea of self-sacrifice in the pursuit of a higher goal; and an appreciation and respect for the transitoriness of life.

The transformation of the samurai from warrior thugs to men of respect and esteem took place after Tokugawa Ieyasu (1543–1616), one of the three great unifiers of Japan, conquered all of Japan and brought an age of peace. After a century of constant battle, the samurai shifted their focus from war to philosophy, art, and the code of honor and service. They were expected to be cultured and literate and admired the ancient saying "bunbu-ryodo" (literary arts, military arts, both ways) or "the pen and the sword in accord." Musashi Miyamoto, my favorite samurai and arguably Japan's greatest swordsman, won sixty-one duels and retired from sword fighting unbeaten, becoming an accomplished artist, sculptor, and calligrapher before his death in 1645. Many of his works are displayed in museums in Japan and throughout the world.

I admired the samurais' balance of the physical with the cerebral. I marveled at their commitment to mastering their craft, to being the best, while also continuing to evolve, as Miyamoto did, to reflect on and appreciate life's beauty. Such duality is inherent in the samurai ideal and is reflected in my own dual interests in athletics and academics as well as in the sciences and the arts.

I was also fascinated with sumo, particularly with the wrestler Taiho, whom many Japanese believe was the greatest Yokozuna (grand champion) of all time. It was not just the match that I enjoyed—which was usually over in seconds—but also the ancient prematch ring rituals, which exemplified the sumo credo of dignity, composure, and dedication.

The highest rank in sumo is Yokozuna, and promotion to that rank requires the highest level of excellence in three areas: power, skill, and dignity/grace. Once this exalted rank is attained—fewer than one hundred wrestlers have achieved it since 1620—a Yokozuna cannot be demoted due to performance. Rather, they are expected to retire if they are not able to uphold the demanding standards of the position and consistently win tournaments. This honorable practice influenced my later stance as university president against tenured faculty who are unproductive, just hanging on, getting paid full time to do no work. I admire the Yokozuna for willingly choosing to not abuse the privilege of their permanent position.

❧

While I was still enthralled with Japanese culture, my nationalistic sentiments must have moderated during the second time I was in first grade. At some point during that year, the family moved to the United States and not only did I not reject Westernization, I couldn't have been more excited.

My dad was about to be stationed at Hanscom Air Force Base, about twenty miles northwest of Boston, Massachusetts. After introducing us to his parents in Ohio and visiting for a few days, he went on to his assignment while we stayed in Ohio. It seems odd now, but at the time I didn't care and didn't question it. After all, he had not been around for the majority of my life.

Before our arrival, I had a complete misunderstanding of what living in the United States was going to be like. I had pictured a big house with open fields full of horses, cows, and chickens. I loved horses—reading the *Black Stallion* series had been my escape to another time and place—and on the fifteen-hour plane ride across the Pacific Ocean, all I could think about was riding one of them.

That wasn't to be. My paternal grandparents lived on the south side of Youngstown, Ohio, in a Black, working-class neighborhood. There were no open fields or animals, not even a dog. At that time, Youngstown was still an important industrial hub that featured the massive furnaces and foundries of such companies as Republic Steel and U.S. Steel. My grandfather, James Sr., worked in the steel mills and had done so his entire adult life. He displayed a tough exterior; he was hard-working and no nonsense. Yet, he flashed an occasional smile that hinted at a kind and gentle soul. Larger than any of his sons, I got my height from him, since I certainly hadn't inherited it from either of my parents.

My grandmother, Lelia, stayed home and raised ten children, including my dad. She understood her role in the family structure—take care of the household, take care of her husband, and take care of her kids—relished it, and never wavered from it. She didn't talk much, and the only activity I ever saw her engage in for enjoyment was going to church.

Sometimes I went with her. I think it was a Baptist church, but the dancing, shouting, and praying out loud during worship were more like what occurs with Pentecostal services. People would get filled with the Holy Spirit and babble incoherently. Occasionally, someone would get so excited they would faint. My favorite part of the service was watching the preacher when he got going. He would start off slow and measured and gradually increase his cadence until he was shouting and speaking in tongues. Sometimes he would remove his jacket and throw it into the congregation. Other times he would take off his glasses and throw them. Whenever we went to church, I would try to guess if it was going to be a jacket or a glasses day.

As was my approach with everything, I tried to understand Christianity and its teachings. I asked a lot of questions but never got satisfactory answers. My mom was a Buddhist at the time, and I was particularly concerned about her having not been "saved" yet and having to go to Hell.

"Can't nice people go to Heaven, too, even if they aren't saved?" I asked my grandmother more than once.

"No," she would reply. "Only those who have been saved."

"Well, what about all the millions of people who haven't even been exposed to Christianity in order to be saved?"

"It doesn't matter, you have to be saved," she would answer.

"If there is only one Jesus, why are there so many Christian denominations? There can only be one true reality so the many different denominations with their different beliefs can't all be correct. Doesn't that mean that some denominations are wrong in their beliefs?"

"You're asking too many questions. Shut up."

The lack of satisfactory answers would nag at me for a long time. I was the type of person who had never believed in Santa Claus because I estimated the number of households in the world and calculated how many global deliveries he could possibly make within a twenty-four-hour span. The numbers didn't add up. I needed rational answers.

On what turned out to be my final visit to church with my grandmother, the preacher took off not only his jacket but also his shoes. I remember because one shoe came flying in my direction and a bunch of people pushed me out of the way to grab it. It was a moving performance, one that prompted my grandmother to jump up out of her seat, raise both hands in the air, and yell "Hallelujah!" at the top of her voice. She then reached into her purse and took out a twenty-dollar bill for the offering basket. It was money that I knew she could not easily spare.

My grandparents had a modest two-bedroom, two-story house with a porch and a partial basement that was just large enough to fit an extra bed as necessary. Besides my grandparents, my uncle Buda and two of my aunts, Darlene and Theresa, lived there when my mom, sister, and I moved in. Darlene had just graduated from high school, Buda was in high school, and Teresa was finishing junior high school.

The room that I remember most vividly is the bathroom, which had a tub with a hose but no shower, as we'd had in Japan. We all had to share this one bathroom and none of us used the tub every day. Coming from Japan, where we bathed either at home or at the public bathhouse daily, I found this apparent cultural difference discomforting.

I went to Monroe Elementary School, which was a two-block walk from the house. After the first month or so, I recall there being discussions as to whether I should skip a grade. I had already made a few friends with kids in my class, though, and my mom didn't want me to have to make new friends so I stayed in the same grade.

꘎

The move to the United States had little effect on my defiant behavior. It just manifested differently than when I was in Japan. In Youngstown, I was the ringleader of a small gang of unruly neighborhood kids, and we were always getting in trouble. I hadn't started off as the ringleader, but I had earned the respect of the other kids by fighting and prevailing against anyone and everyone who challenged me. As a light-skinned kid with long hair, this had happened frequently, until they figured out that it was better if I was with them rather than against them.

In one of the neighborhoods where we roamed, we liked to pull the levers on the fire alarm boxes along the street and watch the fire trucks rush by. One day, as one of my buddies was about to trigger one of them, he noticed that the box looked slightly different and speculated that there was a camera inside. Standing behind him, I scoffed at his reluctance, reached around him, and pulled the lever.

Flashing lights went off accompanied by a siren. We took our seats on the curb and watched as the fire trucks whizzed by. But this time, the trucks were followed by a police car that stopped in front of us. Two cops stepped out and rushed us. We protested that we hadn't pulled the alarm, that they had the wrong boys. After we were handcuffed and searched, one of them responded to our protests by shoving a picture in our faces. Turns out my buddy was right. There was a camera hidden in the alarm and it was his picture that was taken since he was standing in front of me.

Our prank was a serious offense. I don't remember the details, but my friends did not receive any sympathy and were punished accordingly. Because of my good grades, the police deduced that I was not as responsible; apparently, according to them, I just needed a male authoritarian figure in my life. To avoid serious punishment, they worked out a deal with my dad whereby in exchange for leniency for me, the family had to join him in Massachusetts. Until then, we temporarily moved to the northeast side of the city to live with my aunt Norma, her husband, Calvin, and their children, Lynn and Bo. I was not part of the discussions that led to this move, but I can speculate that my unruly behavior contributed to us no longer being welcome in my grandparents' home.

The northeast side was nicer than the south side. The houses were larger and the neighborhood was more upscale. The streets were clean and lined with buckeye trees.

Our cousins were the same age as Dianna and me so it seemed like it could be a good move. It wasn't. This was my second time transferring from school midyear and the adjustment was difficult. Among many peculiarities, all the kids talked about was Ohio State's football team, the Buckeyes, and I had no interest in football at the time.

During one of my first days at Covington Elementary School, sitting alone at recess, I recall the teacher organizing a bunch of classmates to come play with me. I appreciated the effort and went along, but I felt embarrassed that no one wanted to play with me without being forced to do so.

Looking back, I feel fortunate and grateful that my grandparents and Aunt Norma took in my family. Apparently, they had practically no advance warning. My dad didn't keep in contact with his Youngstown family while he was away. Just weeks before we traveled to the United States, he sent a letter to his parents to let them know that he was on his way home with his new family. I realize now that both his parents and his sister Norma were extremely accommodating.

I felt differently as a kid though. Perhaps, because we were the same ages, I perceived that Dianna and I were constantly being compared to Lynn and Bo. And because of my insecurities at the time, it seemed as if we never measured up. They were from the neighborhood and were popular in school whereas we were foreign; they had a stable family structure whereas our dad was some-where many miles away; they had a permanent home whereas we were being shuttled from place to place. At the time, I felt like we were just a bother to everyone.

Our time with Aunt Norma achieved its purpose, though—I didn't get into any more trouble with the police and I wasn't hanging out with my "troublesome" friends. After a few months, we left to join my dad in Massachusetts.

～∂〇

In Massachusetts, we lived in a nice little military-owned house with a fenced-in backyard, beyond which was a wooded area and a large lake. The lake would freeze in the winter and I occasionally ventured out onto the ice. I had a bow and arrow and hunted for rabbits in the woods but never came even close to hitting one. In retrospect, I don't remember much from this time because it was so uneventful, almost peaceful. My family was all together, and I didn't have any run-ins with police, nor did I get into any fights. I went to an on-base military school that was much more integrated and diverse than were the schools in Youngstown. I wasn't such a novelty and didn't have to prove myself all the time.

The only near-skirmish I experienced was when I jumped into the fray to protect a kid who was being bullied. It was after school and a group of kids was picking on another kid who was by himself. After the teasing, one of the kids pushed him. I got into the mix and told the bully to back off. When he didn't, I got into a karate stance, somewhat subconsciously. At the time I did not know martial arts and had only watched movies when in Japan. But I guess it was convincing enough, as I heard whispers from the other kids that I knew karate and the bully backed off.

I don't recall my dad being at the scene, but somehow he knew about it because he mentioned it several times when I was an adult. He remarked that I was always looking out for the weak and vulnerable. I had never heard him say anything positive about me as a child and it made me realize that he was proud of me but didn't know how to express his feelings back then. To this day, I always root for the underdog.

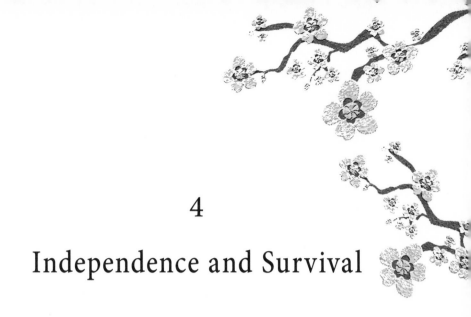

4

Independence and Survival

Although it seemed like much longer, I was in the United States for only a few years. Near the end of 1963, when I was ten, I was pulled out of school—again—and we went back to Japan, this time to Misawa Air Force Base.

I remember the year because it was right before John F. Kennedy was assassinated. Dad, Dianna, and I were in the house when someone came by with the news. Although I knew who President Kennedy was and liked him, I didn't fully comprehend the historic significance of the event until I witnessed my dad's reaction. Initially stunned and disbelieving, his expression gradually changed to one of despair. It was as if all his bottled-up hopes for a better society were suddenly shattered. Dad loved JFK.

Another unforgettable event occurred a few months later when Cassius Clay, who later changed his name to Muhammad Ali, beat Sonny Liston. The next day, my fourth-grade classmates and I were shadowboxing during recess—some of us disbelieving that the invincible Sonny Liston could possibly have been beaten, but all of us marveling at the confidence and bravado of the loudmouthed but talented Clay—when a group of sixth-grade boys started hassling us. For whatever reason, the hassling turned into a fight between one of the sixth graders and me. Though I got in some good shots, he eventually put me in a headlock. Because I was unable to maneuver, my face was an easy target as he pummeled it over and over. When a teacher finally came out and broke it up, I was relieved but embarrassed. I didn't lose many fights. The most humiliating part was my black eye, a visible sign of my defeat.

Shortly afterward, resolved to never let that happen again, I began taking judo classes with a traditional, Japanese instructor who wore a red belt, signifying that he possessed a 9th or 10th degree black belt. Judo, and to some extent baseball, provided me a much-needed sense of focus and purpose. I excelled in both, achieving the rank of shodan (1st degree black belt) in judo in four years and making the little league all-star team as a pitcher and first baseman. As nothing else in my life was very positive at the time, I poured myself into both sports.

During our time in Misawa, which lasted from when I was ten to almost fifteen, we lived about two or three miles from the base, address G-23. It was probably not a military house, as we had few, if any, American neighbors. Our house was on a dirt road that was always muddy after it rained. At night, it was very dark as there were no streetlights. Within a block or two were a public bathhouse and a small local grocery store owned by an elderly Japanese couple.

During these years, my mom's gambling problem became more pronounced. If there was any question as to whether she was addicted during the early Yakuza years, there was now no doubt. She went on gambling binges for days and weeks, occasionally even months at a time. Reminiscent of our Youngstown experience, my dad was also frequently gone. He was stationed in other places, particularly Vietnam, for long stints of time and would come back to visit periodically. Sometimes Mom was home but not Dad; sometimes Dad was home but not Mom. Occasionally, they were both home but that didn't happen very often. Most of the time, Dianna and I were alone.

Since I was five years older than Dianna, I was responsible for her well-being. I made sure that she had clean clothes to wear and that she went to school. It was also up to me to shop at the local grocery store, where we had an account. To call the store a "grocery store" may give the wrong impression. It was a small local store with rice, fruit, and vegetables. There were no frozen items, except perhaps ice, there were no canned goods, and there certainly were no "TV dinners" or other prepared food items.

We didn't have many neighbors, nor did we have many friends outside of school. No one seemed to know that a ten-year-old and a five-year-old were living on their own, or maybe they just didn't care. We developed a routine of sorts and somehow managed.

When we first moved, Dianna was too young for school and so she stayed home by herself during the day when Mom was not around. When she turned six, she started school on base. Although a school bus took us back and forth from home, I usually walked home because of judo practice and other after-school activities. At an age when most kids can't boil water, Dianna prepared and cooked Japanese rice—not instant rice or Rice-A-Roni—and would usually have some ready by the time I came home. After eating, we would both do our homework.

The Japanese have a special relationship with rice, which is considered a national treasure. Rice cultivation began about three thousand years ago and became a foundation of Japan's national identity. Mom was very particular about her rice. She wouldn't even touch it unless it was a specific type cooked a specific way on the stovetop, not in a rice cooker. Like Mom, Dianna would wash and soak the rice and watch over it as it cooked on the stovetop.

Occasionally, if I was really tired and hungry and had some money, I would stop by the tiny ramen shop on the way home. Walking in, I would be greeted with a shout of "irasshaimase," meaning "welcome, please come in." The flames of the stoves and the boiling water emitted warmth, the smell of the broth brewed for hours or even days permeated the air, and the sound of patrons slurping their noodles would bring a smile to my face. Very few things capture the spirit of Japan as does a perfect bowl of ramen, and both my soul and body would be replenished as I left to complete the journey home. Ramen is still my favorite comfort food.

We had another responsibility: caring for a dog named Frisky that we had taken in from the streets. After Frisky became pregnant, Dianna and I watched with trepidation as each little pup came out of her. We were just kids, alone and unsure of how we could assist. It was a small litter, and one of the pups died after a few days. We struggled just taking care of ourselves. Realizing that we could not provide the attention the remaining pups needed to survive, I found homes for them.

One evening, when we got home, Mom met us at the door and told us that Frisky had been hit by a car in front of our house. When we saw our dog, she was in obvious distress, taking shallow breaths and whimpering constantly. We went to school the next day with the expectation of burying her when we came home. But when we returned home that day, Mom informed us that the Korean owner of the laundry down the street had taken her. Mom had told us stories of Koreans eating dog; it occurred to both of us that maybe that's what happened to Frisky. Mom never mentioned whether Frisky was alive or dead when she was taken. The thought of Frisky being eaten was unbearable, and we didn't want to know. As much as we enjoyed having Mom home, it occurred to us that Frisky would have avoided that fate had she been gone.

Most of the time, it was up to us to deal with whatever emergencies arose. Misawa is located in the northern part of Japan and it snowed a lot in the winter. One day, Dianna fell on the ice in front of our house and split her head. The cut was high on her forehead near her hairline, and blood was spurting out. Unable to stop the bleeding, I had no choice but to take her to the emergency room of a hospital. The military hospital on base was too far so we made our way to the local Japanese hospital. It was still a long walk, and it was dark. The bleeding was bad, and I sensed that I had to get her to the hospital as quickly as possible.

I walked briskly and Dianna was lagging behind. "Dianna, keep up," I pleaded. "The blood is up to your ankle and rising." My admonition was medically nonsensical, but she was struggling and all I could think about was getting her to the hospital. I picked her up and carried her for a while but it was slippery and I couldn't maintain a good pace. After setting her down to walk again, I exhorted, "It's up to your knees now, Dianna. We've got to get to the hospital before the blood gets to your ears." I saw a quizzical look on her face as if she was trying to understand what would happen if the blood reached her ears. In a final moment of desperation, I yelled, "If it reaches your ears, it will be too late to save you." This must have made an impression because I've heard her recount this story many times since.

When we made it to the hospital, I had to explain why neither of our parents had accompanied us. I had no money and no health insurance to cover the cost of the visit. The hospital likely required some sort of payment, but whatever I said must have worked since Dianna was treated. Looking back, I'm not sure why no one at the hospital looked into why two kids were seeking medical care without a supervising adult, but Dianna was released to my care.

When we lived in Misawa, I saw Dianna through many of the typical travails of childhood. One time she had a wiggly tooth that was causing her discomfort. I tied a string around it and secured the string to a doorknob. Apprehension was written all over Dianna's face, but before she could object I slammed the door shut and cleanly dislodged the tooth.

Dianna didn't cry. She had a big grin as she took the tooth and carefully put it away. Later that night, I saw her retrieve the tooth and tuck it under her pillow before she went to sleep, fully anticipating the tooth fairy's arrival by morning. Knowing that the tooth fairy was not coming, I was heartbroken as I went to bed. One of my prized possessions was my baseball card collection. Since I didn't have Japanese yen and didn't want Dianna to be disappointed that the tooth fairy had not come, I woke up early and exchanged my baseball cards for the tooth under her pillow.

All kids should be able to experience the wonder of tooth fairies and other fantastical folklore. When Dianna woke up and peered under the pillow, she exclaimed, "Look, Roy! I have baseball cards, just like you." In all likelihood, that moment was probably the only typical childhood experience she had.

In truth, I was not always a good brother. Once, Dianna needed a sheet of paper to do her homework. Instead of just giving it to her, I struck a deal with her that she would have to give me half her dinner when Mom cooked. She had to surreptitiously slip food to me under the dinner table without being detected. This was just mean since I don't recall having a shortage of food, and I probably could have gotten another portion just by asking.

Another time, after watching a movie in which someone was hanged with a rope, I talked Dianna into trying an experiment in which I tied a rope around her neck and had her stand on a chair. I was just about to kick the chair from under her when—fortunately—Mom came home and walked in. I can't imagine now what I was thinking, but I don't believe that I intended to harm her or that I was being cruel. Unsupervised kids sometimes do stupid things and no one was there to curtail my curiosity. Notwithstanding a few such lapses, I was usually a good brother and tried to take care of her.

There was always uncertainty as to whether our parents would be home for Christmas. Usually they were not. But I do remember one Christmas when I was about twelve or thirteen when Dad was home. I had bought him a Christmas present with some of the money my mom had left me. Being too shy to present it, I asked Dianna to give it to him from both of us on Christmas Eve. Dad was surprised by the gift, which I no longer remember, and didn't know how to respond. He acted as if it was not a big deal, but I could tell he was overwhelmed by the gesture. Dianna was joyous and coaxed him out of his shell as she jumped up and down on one end of the couch as he sat at the other. I sat in a corner, quietly watching the two of them immersed in holiday celebration. I didn't join in the revelry, but I experienced an inner contentment that had always eluded me every holiday season. I missed Mom but went to bed happy.

Dianna and I woke up the next morning still feeling great. As we walked out of our bedroom, we saw something that stopped us in our tracks. Beside a fully decorated—albeit synthetic—Christmas tree that Dad had put up while we slept were two bikes: a red ten-speed for me and a smaller blue bike for Dianna. I rubbed my eyes to make sure I was seeing properly. I was emotionally overwhelmed. The bike was the first, and only, Christmas present I can remember ever receiving as a child. To this day, I have a special relationship with bikes.

To be clear, I did see my parents periodically. Mom would show up unexpectedly from time to time, although never when Dad was home. When she did show up, it was usually late at night and we would not know of her return until we were awakened for breakfast. The sight of her sitting at the breakfast table, smiling in front of hot food, would fill me with happiness, and life would resume with some semblance of normalcy for a while. Sometimes, she would come back just to check on us, settle the incurred debt at the grocery store, leave me with a stash of money, and take off again; other times, she would stay long enough that my hopes would be raised that she was home to stay.

My mom had a gambling buddy, Obatta-san, who would often accompany her on these brief visits home. Obatta-san was also married and had three daughters. One of them had a heart condition and was sickly. As with my mom, there seemed to be an intensity of purpose about Obatta-san's gambling. He was a nice guy and I believe that he genuinely wanted to take good care of his family. He probably dreamed of hitting it big. Unfortunately, as is typical with gambling, the intermittent high of winning is invariably overcome by the despair of losing more than can be afforded.

One day, Obatta-san's wife stopped by with the girls. With tears in her eyes, she profusely thanked my mom for her support of Obatta-san and for making sure that her family was provided for. I do not know what my mom had done, but she was a very generous person. When she had money, she would share freely. My guess is that she extended that largesse to Obatta-san's wife and family when Obatta-san was in a downward spiral of debt.

My dad's homecomings were also unexpected, at least for me. Usually, though not always, my mother was home, so she must have anticipated his returns. During these times, family life seemed almost normal. Mom would cook, and we would all have dinner together. My favorite dishes at the time were fried pork chops and meat loaf. I would do my homework, go to bed at a specified time, and read for several additional hours with a flashlight under the blankets.

These times when both Mom and Dad were home were not idyllic. In fact, it was during one of these periods that I was sexually abused. In truth, my first sexual experience had occurred a few years earlier in Youngstown with an older girl who took advantage of my inexperience and naivete. But she was just a teenager, and I rationalized that what occurred was not sexual abuse, though it actually was. This time it was with an adult, and there could be no question that it was abuse.

When my parents went out together, they often hired a babysitter. I always found this odd since Dianna and I were alone most of the time anyway, with Mom away gambling and Dad on military assignment. The babysitter, who was Japanese, seemed really nice around my parents and around Dianna. When alone with me, she was a monster. She would distract Dianna with television or with games and would take me into my parents' bedroom. She would present me with a choice: have sex with her or be locked in the closet. The first time, I chose the closet. Dark and cramped, the closet had a lock and there was no way out. I thought about shouting for help but didn't want to alarm Dianna. Besides, I was her big brother and I didn't want my little sister coming to the rescue.

After that first time in the closet, I chose sex. I wonder now why I couldn't have just overpowered her and resisted, or why I didn't tell my parents what was happening. But for some reason, I didn't. Like many victims of abuse, I was probably afraid of confronting my abuser. Neither of my parents had been a dependable presence in my life, and I had no reason to believe that I would be supported if I told on the babysitter. The consequence of staying quiet was more predictable, so that's what I did.

The babysitter didn't bother Dianna. But Dianna had her own battles with sexual abuse.

One such situation was with Mr. Lincoln, who was a friend of the family. He was a Black man who became a Buddhist. Mr. Lincoln would come around the house a lot. At first it was only when my parents were home, but over time he started dropping by when they were away. I noticed that he would follow Dianna around, particularly when he thought I was preoccupied and not paying attention. Once, when Dianna and I were alone, the phone rang and she answered it. Her mood changed and she became anxious. At her request, I picked up another line and listened as this pervert made sexual innuendos. I became incensed and yelled that I would beat him up with a baseball bat if I ever saw him again. That was the last time we heard from him.

Mr. Lincoln wasn't the only grown man who sexually harassed or assaulted her. Sadly, there were many. One of them was the father of one of her friends who lived nearby. Dianna stopped going over to their house, which deprived her of one of the only childhood friendships she had. When I found out, I blamed myself for not being more observant and doing a better job of protecting her.

Back then, I didn't think much of my parents' negligence in not confronting these perpetrators. Consistent with their general parenting approach, I believed that they were just oblivious to what was going on in plain sight. I no longer believe that to have been the case, at least for Mom. Years later, when we first moved to the United States, Dianna was molested by a much older distant relative on Dad's side of the family and she told Mom. Inexplicably, Mom did not confront the molester. I still have a difficult time reconciling this response to Dianna's plight.

My dad was the type of person who focused on the negatives rather than the positives, particularly, it seemed, when it came to me. One example in particular immediately comes to mind. On the first day of sixth grade, I stood at the school bus stop feeling excited and a bit anxious: excited because it was lonely having just Dianna around all summer and I would be around my classmates again; anxious because I didn't have any new school clothes. Wearing his military uniform, Dad got out of a taxi and walked toward me, a duffel bag slung over his shoulder. I hadn't seen him all summer. Without a "Hi" or a "How you doing" or just about anything else most people would say after not being around for months, he asked, "Why you wearing blue socks with black pants?" With the exception of occasional visits by my mom, both my parents had been absent for most of the summer. During that entire time, I had made sure Dianna and I were clothed and fed. Unlike all the other school kids, neither of us had new school clothes to start the year. In fact, I had spent the previous day washing and ironing so that we at least had something clean to wear. And all he could comment on was the color of my socks! To this day, I am conscious of the color of men's socks in relation to the color of their pants. I actually don't wear blue or black socks anymore, just multicolored ones.

The few times my dad was home, our only interaction was through sports. He enjoyed sports and had participated in boxing during the early years of his military service. Dad was a middleweight, which would have put his weight minimum at 165.3 pounds. Even as he aged, he worked out and stayed in shape, never weighing much more than 175 pounds.

After school and judo practice, during the long walk home, I would often dream of food to settle my hunger pains. But instead of serving dinner, my dad would be waiting for me with a catcher's mitt on, and we would go to a baseball field that was two or three blocks away. To this day, I don't know if he considered this quality time or if he was simply drilling me to be the best. Perhaps it was both. Whatever his intentions, I would pitch to him for what seemed like hours. I had a wicked curveball for a little league pitcher, but my preference was to throw as hard as I could, trying to knock him backward on his butt, or at least to make sure his catching hand stung. Dinner was afterward.

Unless I was behind in my homework, I usually concluded my day with a bath at the sento. Most Americans take a shower in the morning to wash and prepare for the day, and we certainly had a shower in our house. But in Japan, baths are about more than simply getting clean, and most Japanese take baths at the public bathhouse at the end of the day. Although washing the body is part of the ritual, Japanese baths are as much about relaxation and rejuvenating the body and spirit. The local sento I frequented had three large soaking tubs that ranged in temperature from very hot to extremely hot to scalding hot. I would always start by soaking in the very hot tub and then progress to the extremely hot one. Depending on the level of redness of the burnt skin on the men coming out of the scalding hot tub, I sometimes ventured into this one also. Soaking in the hot water with my eyes closed, I would get lost in deep contemplation and forget my day-to-day struggles.

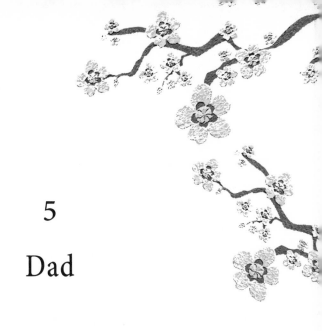

5

Dad

My dad was born in Youngstown on November 27, 1929, in the middle of the pack of four brothers and five sisters. Three of his brothers also enlisted in the military after high school. I once asked him why they all went to the military rather than go to college. He commented that college didn't seem like a realistic option at the time; it was either work in the steel mills, like his father, or enlist in the military. Located within a ten-minute drive from where he grew up was Youngstown State University. The fact that it was inaccessible to him is a sad commentary on the state of public higher education for Blacks in the 1940s and 1950s. As president of a public university located in a poor, predominantly Black city, not unlike Youngstown in many ways, I often reflect on his comment.

I'm not sure why my dad was not around during my early childhood in Japan and in Youngstown. He was quiet and somewhat secretive. One incident at a pachinko parlor in downtown Misawa was particularly puzzling. One late afternoon, I was walking home when I spotted him in town, standing by an intersection. When I went over to greet him, he acted strangely, almost as if he didn't know me. There was a pachinko parlor on the street corner and he told me to follow him as he went in. I found this odd since my dad was not a gambler and did not play pachinko (a mechanical game with elements of both a slot machine and pinball). Once inside, he kept his distance and did not look directly at me. He was fidgety and acted as if he was searching for something or someone, but it was obviously feigned. I felt as if I was an impediment to whatever it was he was doing. After a while, I just left. To this day, I wonder what that was really all about.

My dad also had some good qualities, which became more evident as he got older. But, during my years growing up, his frugality and alcoholism are the overriding traits seared into my memory. Although I'm sure he could have afforded it, we never owned a home. We always lived in rented apartments, and our furniture was always the type that could be considered "temporary" until something nicer and more permanent was purchased. Except that he never got around to purchasing the permanent furniture. Dad never owned a new car and would never think of leasing one. He would pay cash for an inexpensive car and his nephew Floyd, an auto mechanic, would keep it running in good shape. He paid for everything with cash. He didn't even have a credit card until much later in life.

We sometimes took road trips to visit his family in Youngstown or his sister Irene in Virginia, but other than that, we never took vacations. He was always saving money for retirement, for when he and my mom could travel the world together. She died at a relatively young age, when she was only fifty-four. Mom never got to go on any of these vacations; my dad had all this money saved up but no one to spend it with.

I recall receiving a letter when I was in high school from a residential basketball camp informing me that they had denied my request to clean and wash dishes in lieu of paying the camp enrollment fee. I had never sent such a request and was enraged that my dad had sent it on my behalf without my knowledge. More than angry, though, I was embarrassed. How could he possibly think that I could clean and wash dishes for a bunch of guys that I also had to play basketball with? Besides, it was a three- or four-day camp and the fee was modest, something like ninety dollars. If I had wanted to attend, I could have paid the fee myself from money I earned flipping hamburgers at the military snack bar where I worked on weekends.

My dad didn't understand my angry reaction, which makes me believe that he had good intentions. He was just very frugal; it wouldn't occur to him to pay for something if there was a way to get it for free.

Dad was an alcoholic. When I became an adult—and particularly after my medical training—I would try to get him to understand that he had a drinking problem. But as with most alcoholics, he refused the label and came up with excuses for his behavior, claiming he could stop any time he wanted. "I get up for work every day and am not sitting on the street corner drinking Ripple from a brown paper bag," he would retort.

His abuse of alcohol affected his military career and our family's well-being. Even as a child, I knew that he was passed over for promotions because of alcohol-related incidents. My dad retired from the military as a staff sergeant (four stripes), though enlisted men in the Air Force at the time could earn up to eight stripes plus various additional symbols signifying even higher ranks. At least once that I know of, but perhaps more often, he earned a fifth stripe but got demoted down to four because of drunken driving resulting in personal injury to someone. Most of the guys I played basketball with in Misawa were enlisted men, and although they were just a few years older than me, even they had three or four stripes.

After spending his entire adult life in the military, my dad retired around 1970, while I was still in high school, and got a job sorting mail at the federal post office in downtown Washington, D.C. When he worked the weekend night shift, I would drop him off, keep the car, and then pick him back up after work.

Dad was not an obnoxious drunk. Rather, people described him as being very likable when he was drinking. Although he was shy socially, drinking made him gregarious, the life of the party. People loved it when he came around and would exclaim, "Wilson is here!" But he didn't know when to stop, and there would always be a point when his sociability became annoying, at least from my perspective and that of my mom. We never left any social gathering that included alcohol when it was the appropriate time to leave. There was always one last drink. This habit was a point of contention with my mom, and it was embarrassing for me.

I never saw my dad drink alcohol alone. It was a social thing for him. When I was in high school, I would borrow his car on weekends to party and hang out with my friends. When he wasn't working, I would drop him off at the apartment where his nephew Willie James lived with his girlfriend, Mirline. Along with Willie James's brother, Floyd, the auto mechanic, they would drink Johnnie Walker Black Label scotch all night until I picked him up, usually well past midnight. I liked the arrangement because I was able to have his car for the night, and it kept him from driving while drunk.

My relationship with my dad was not healthy, especially when I was a kid. Like a drug addict needing his fix, I needed something from my dad that he could not provide. Perhaps, subconsciously, I felt abandoned and wanted to be acknowledged by him. Whatever the reason, I craved his approval and tried to excel in everything I did. But no matter how much I excelled, it was never good enough and his approval was always elusive.

When I was eleven, I played in a series of baseball games against one of Japan's top little league teams from Tokyo that determined who would progress toward the Little League World Series. It was a three-game series and I was to pitch the first game and potentially the third. We won the first match in a close 2–1 pitchers' game. I had pitched a great game. Further, winning the first game meant that we were guaranteed a third game and that I would likely be called to pitch again.

My dad was usually a quiet, reserved person—unless he had been drinking—but he was boisterous at my baseball games. He had his opinions and was not shy about expressing them. On the drive home, I made some comment about the next game. I was really excited for our win and had expected that he would be also. Instead, he clutched the steering wheel and looked straight ahead as if he couldn't bear to speak to me. "If I was the coach," he said, "I wouldn't play you tomorrow. You didn't get a hit, not even a single one." Yet again, despite my earlier high, I felt that I had fallen short.

His criticism was not limited to sports performance; it also extended to academics. I was a good student and generally received As with an occasional A minus. An A minus was not good enough. "How come you didn't get an A?"

would be his comment. Only occasionally did he stand in my corner. Once, in seventh grade, my English teacher, Ms. Rinehart, gave me a B on an assignment, though all my answers were correct. She had downgraded me because I was careless with the heading and wrote down the wrong date. When I explained this to Dad, he came to school to speak to Ms. Rinehart. Although she stood her ground and refused to change my grade, I felt proud that my dad had advocated for me.

Furthermore, the incident taught me a lesson. Ms. Rinehart was hard on me, not because she didn't like me but because she believed that I was not performing to my potential, and she often downgraded me because of carelessness. She taught me the importance of paying close attention to detail, to be deliberate and careful, a practice that would later prove vital in microscopic eye surgery.

It wasn't until after college that my relationship with my dad changed. The turning point came the weekend of my graduation from Allegheny College in the spring of 1976. In just a few months, I would be starting medical school at Harvard. My parents had driven up from Maryland to see me graduate. The only other time they had come to Allegheny was when they dropped me off four years earlier.

I had performed well at Allegheny and had developed special relationships with several of my professors. They had high regard for me and were effusive in their praise when they met my parents. Since I was the first in our extended family to go to college, my mom and dad didn't know what to expect and were overwhelmed by the pomp and circumstance of the celebratory events. I was in all the honor societies, and each one had its own invitation-only graduation celebration. At one of them, the Phi Beta Kappa honor society, my dad learned the secret handshake. He could not have been prouder. The next day, after all the celebrations had concluded and it was time to leave campus, Dad gave me *the* handshake and then surprised me with a big hug. I was twenty-two years old, and this was the first time he had ever embraced me.

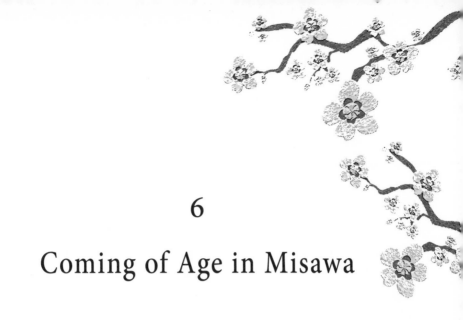

6

Coming of Age in Misawa

I was physically precocious in middle school and spent most of my non-school time playing basketball and hanging out at the gym with the GIs.

Misawa's combination middle and high school was small and included grades seven through twelve. I was there for seventh and eighth grades and played soccer in the fall, played basketball in the winter, and ran track in the spring. At about 5′10″, I was tall for my age. I had good "hops" and could occasionally coax the ball through the rim for a dunk. Had I kept growing, I undoubtedly would have been a power forward, but my growth spurt slowed. Peaking at about 6′2″, I played the shooting guard position in high school and college.

It's not that I didn't like being with the other middle school kids, but I thought the GIs were cool and I admired the camaraderie they had with each other. Jimmy Stewart and I were in the same grade. He was a couple of inches taller than me and was an outstanding ballplayer. He played with the GIs also, so we hung out together a lot. I also had a casual friendship with several girls from school—Gwen Vidinha, Pat Utsumi, JoAnne Wood, and Debbie Sundloff—and we sometimes socialized at the bowling alley or the Teen Club.

The Teen Club had dances, usually with a band, on weekends. It was also a place to gather with friends, shoot pool, or play Ping-Pong. There may have been a small fee to join, and there was an initiation for membership. That, I remember distinctly.

Around the time I turned thirteen, I was in the pool room with a friend who was also a new member candidate. All of a sudden, a group of older teenagers came in and pinned us on the ground and blindfolded us. Suddenly, I felt something cold and wet on my belly. From the smell, I could tell that it was mustard and ketchup. I didn't like the sensation of being smeared with wet condiments, but understanding that it was an initiation prank, I tried to be good-natured about it. Then I felt something smothering my face and heard laughter. When they let me up and I took off the blindfold, I realized that one of the guys had dropped his pants and sat on my face. There was absolutely no chance that I would let someone sit their nasty butt on my face without retaliating. Enraged, I took a pool stick and swung it across the back of his head. He, of course, fought back, and we engaged in an all-out fight until it was broken up by one of the staff.

My membership at the Teen Club was delayed for a few weeks due to the incident, but eventually I became a member. I thought about not joining but the base was small and there was not much else to do if I wanted to see my teenage friends outside of school. Besides, the other new member candidate, who was white, had experienced the same treatment so the prank was probably not racially motivated. He convinced me to let it go. I moved on but never forgot that incident, and the memory of it is the reason I never joined a college fraternity. I had resolved to never again go through any sort of initiation rite that involved hazing or other stupid stuff.

The Teen Club was a good place to socialize with my schoolmates on weekends, but it was basically an all-white group, and I didn't feel the same camaraderie I did with the GIs. The late 1960s was a time of social and political unrest around the world. In America, the Civil Rights Act of 1964 prohibited discrimination in hiring, promoting, and firing, but social life was still very segregated. Black pride and Black Power salutes were coming into fashion, as well as Afros and the Black Is Beautiful movement. There weren't many Black teenagers in Misawa and, besides Jimmy, I don't recall having any Black friends my age. In contrast, all of the GIs I played ball with were Black. We called each other "brothers" and the women were called "sapphires." Although "sapphires" had a negative connotation—the centuries-old stereotype of the angry and emasculating Black woman—we used it as a compliment, to denote a woman who was beautiful and cherished, like the blue stone.

This was a time of soul music. While my schoolmates were jumping up and down to the California surfer anthem "Wipe Out" by the Ventures at the Teen Club, the GIs were mellowing to the sweet sounds of "My Girl" by the Temptations. The GIs had cool names—many just went by their initials. The GI I was closest to was G.O. He lifted weights when he was not playing ball and would often quip that he was like the muscle car, GTO (Pontiac) minus the T. All the GI brothers walked with a well-cultivated strut, similar to a limp, and wore swagger sunglasses, even at night. When they weren't playing ball or in their military uniforms, they were always dressed to impress. Their suits were stylish and custom-made with the finest materials, usually mohair or natural silk. The shoes they wore were called "half a hundreds" because they cost fifty dollars, a hefty sum for enlisted men in the 1960s.

The term "Black Power" as a social and racial slogan gained traction during this time. One of the movement's spokespeople, Malcolm X, argued that Blacks needed to build power on their own, rather than seek accommodations from the power structure in place. A migration from a philosophy of nonviolence to one of greater militancy culminated in the founding of the Black Panther Party in October 1966.

Privately, many of my GI friends embraced the Black Panther Party and its philosophy. It was against this backdrop that a Black consciousness was awakened in me. Music and style were one thing, but the movement was about so much more. Racial pride by itself was meaningless without economic sufficiency, equality, and political influence. G.O. would always tell me: "Hey Youngblood, make sure you study, get good grades, go to college. Education is the one thing no one can ever take away from you." When he felt more radical, he would warn about the potential of a race war and explain that rhetoric and guns were useless and that knowledge alone was the weapon of choice. "Youngblood, you've got to get as much knowledge as possible and use that against the white man. That's the only chance we got."

During this time, I noticed another dynamic that was at least partly race related. The military was segregated by rank, with facilities for officers to live and socialize separate from those for GIs. *The officers' facilities were nicer.* There were even rules against officers fraternizing with enlisted soldiers. And if a GI encountered an officer, he had to show respect by saluting.

Dad was a GI. In fact, every Black soldier I knew was a GI, and all the officers I knew were white. I had never even seen a Black officer. My observation at the time was that since the higher-ranked officers had nicer facilities than the GIs and commanded more respect, whites were more privileged. Of course, there was nothing inherent about race that led one to become an officer. I learned that the determining factor was a college degree. And so I decided that I would go to college.

Another sort of consciousness was awakened in me during this time. Since I lived off base and spoke Japanese fairly well, I spent a lot of time in the Japanese business community. My mom would leave me money so that I could take care of basic needs for Dianna and me, and so I was often shopping in town. The experience gave me a clear understanding of why Americans visiting foreign countries are sometimes labeled "ugly Americans." It embarrassed me to see American military personnel being loud and belligerent because a Japanese business owner could not speak English well. I was embarrassed not only for the Japanese man or woman who had to endure the abuse but also by the sense of entitlement and arrogance displayed by my fellow Americans. We were on their land, in their country. What right did we have to expect the Japanese to speak our language? If anything, shouldn't we have been speaking *their* language if we ventured off base and did business with them?

I often tried to intervene in these situations and offered to interpret. Both parties were almost always appreciative and got what they needed from the subsequent transaction. But occasionally, the American would get even more belligerent and rant that the United States had conquered the Japanese and they needed to speak English.

There is a joke that is often told in global circles that goes like this: What do you call a person who speaks three languages? *Trilingual.* What do you call a person who speaks two languages? *Bilingual.* What do you call a person who speaks just one language? *American.*

I lament the fact that I can no longer speak Japanese well and have become one of those Americans who speak only one language. Throughout her life, my mom spoke to me exclusively in Japanese. When she died, I didn't have many opportunities to practice the language, so I've lost most of my vocabulary, beyond the ability to order in a Japanese restaurant, which doesn't really count. Nevertheless, I feel fortunate to have been fluent in two languages and deeply connected to another culture. My interest in global health was nurtured by my knowledge of and experience living within another culture. In turn, my receptivity toward other cultures has allowed me to appreciate, respect, and value differences between populations of people, which has greatly enriched my life.

My school years in Misawa were certainly my coming-of-age. At an earlier time, I was immersed in Japanese culture and was fascinated by it. During this period, I established my identity as a Black male. How biracial kids identify racially is dependent on many influences, including the assignment of race at birth and one's lived experience in a racialized society. In my case, I was heavily influenced by my relationship with Black GIs during an explosive period of Black awakening in America.

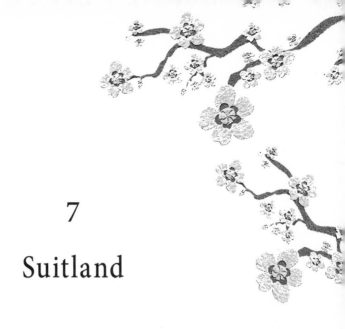

7

Suitland

I came back to the United States the summer before ninth grade when my dad got stationed at Andrews Air Force Base in Prince George County, Maryland, near the border of southeast Washington, D.C. We lived about twenty minutes away in Suitland, in an apartment complex called Shady Grove. My new school, Suitland High School, enrolled kids predominantly from a lower-middle-class socioeconomic background and was very integrated; about a third to half of the student body was Black and the remainder white. I don't recall that there were any Asians. The school was not strong academically, but it had highly regarded athletics. On its Wikipedia page, seven of the ten people identified as notable alumni are professional football players. I played football and basketball and ran track, mainly the 100-yard sprint.

All of my friends were Black and were from the neighborhood, living in either Shady Grove or other nearby apartment complexes. It would be fair to say that school was not among their highest priorities. They liked to hang out on street corners and sing a cappella. I couldn't carry a tune so I didn't join. They also enjoyed getting high a lot, usually by smoking marijuana or sniffing glue. I smoked marijuana a few times but didn't like it because it made me feel paranoid and not in total control of myself. As for sniffing glue and other drugs, my friends never pressured me and, in fact, insisted I not join in. They were being protective because I was an athlete, a gesture I greatly appreciated.

They had my back in other ways as well. Our relationship was cemented during the early days of living at Shady Grove when they assisted me in confronting Billy, a Suitland High dropout and leader of a small group of redneck thugs at Shady Grove. Billy was a bully and braggard. He was also very insecure.

One day during that first summer at Shady Grove, before school had even started, a group of us headed to the basketball court. Billy was one of those all-talk-no-action guys, and he was fishing for compliments on how good he was on the court. We ended up on opposite teams, and for some reason he wanted to match up against me. Embarrassed and frustrated after I dunked on him, he threw a punch at me. I was able to deflect the punch and throw him to the ground with a judo move. Nothing more happened; we resumed playing, and I just forgot about it.

A few weeks later, when I was walking in the neighborhood, Billy sucker punched me from behind. He made up some excuse for why he had been thrown on the ground previously and challenged me to a fight. As I got into a fighting stance, I suddenly sensed that he was not alone. I was surrounded by four or five of his white buddies closing in with smirks on their faces. After sizing up the situation, I bolted. With my heart beating so hard that I could hear it, I am sure that I've never run faster, either before or since—and I ran a 10.1-second 100-yard dash in high school track. After about 50 yards of an all-out sprint, I found yet another gear and sped up even more.

I didn't slow down until I saw my new acquaintances. After I explained the situation to them, they walked me back to where Billy and his thugs were hanging out. They kept the thugs in check as I challenged Billy one-on-one. But Billy came up with yet another lame excuse as to why he couldn't fight. However, word traveled widely and no one from the neighborhood ever bothered me again.

Several years later, my football coach pulled me aside during preseason practice to let me know that he did not approve of my friends. As a white man, he had stereotyped them as lazy drugheads, and he warned me that they would negatively influence my hard work and commitment on the field. Believing his characterization to be untrue and unfair, I defended them; but he demanded that I stop associating with them, even giving me a veiled threat if I did not.

That night, I pondered my dilemma. I was a starter for the team and I loved playing. Yet, there were some principles that transcended personal considerations. Loyalty was chief among them. The next day, I quit the team. I rationalized that I needed to begin focusing more exclusively on basketball anyway if I was going to get an athletic scholarship to go to college. But the true reason was that my friends stuck by me and I was going to stick by them.

In the late 1960s and early 1970s, many Washington, D.C., neighborhoods were in the early stages of gentrification, and Black families were being displaced to nearby suburbs like Suitland where rents were substantially lower. The Anders brothers were among those who moved to Shady Grove apartments. The younger brother, Isaac, was in my grade and we met on the local basketball court, the same court where I had schooled Billy. Isaac was a good playground player and we would go around looking for games at area courts throughout southeast D.C. He was short, probably about 5'8", but could dunk the ball and had a nice jumper.

Unfortunately, although he played junior varsity for a year, he was cut trying out for varsity. Our relationship had been built exclusively on basketball, so we drifted apart. At the same time, I started hanging out with his older brother, Eddie, who had attended Anacostia High School, although I doubt he graduated. Eddie was intimately familiar with the D.C. scene and we had a lot of fun together. One of our favorite pastimes was to slowly cruise along the strip of road that ran through the park that flanked the Anacostia River, watching the people who were lined along the road barbequing and blaring loud music. It was always a scene. Locals referred to us young guys as river rats, a name we proudly bore.

Eddie and I established a mutually beneficial arrangement. Eddie didn't have transportation, but he had a steady girlfriend who went to Anacostia. I had access to my dad's car. When we hung out, Eddie would have his transportation and I would have a date from among his girlfriend's friends. It was a great system.

We partied a lot. Every weekend, Eddie would have a list of addresses of house parties throughout the city and we would try to go to three or four of them. This was fine for Eddie, who didn't go to school or work, but it took a toll on me.

The summer between tenth grade and eleventh was particularly difficult. I was playing in the Jelleff League, a summer basketball league made up of high school all-star players. I was also seeing a young woman who lived and worked in downtown D.C. I had met Debbie at one of the house parties I went to with Eddie. The first thing I would typically do at these parties was check out the girls, but I didn't see her until she asked if I wanted to dance. Caught off guard, I wasn't very cool, but I recovered and we ended up dating. Debbie had gone to community college for a few years down South somewhere and came to D.C. to work in a government job. She was also a talented artist and her tiny apartment on 14th Street NW was cramped with canvases in various stages of completion. I'm not sure what she saw in a high school guy, but if I wasn't hanging with Eddie, I was usually with her. On top of all that, I worked at a café for military personnel on Andrews Air Force Base and often did the night shift or even a double shift. After all, I had to have money to buy my stylish clothes.

Then, early in eleventh grade, I met two people who influenced my life trajectory more than anyone to that point and perhaps even thereafter. One became my first love, the other my academic mentor and coach.

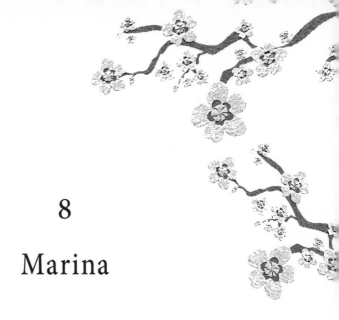

8

Marina

I was in tenth grade when I first saw Marina at a pep rally held in Suitland's gymnasium. When she got up to walk across the floor, all the students stopped whatever they were doing to watch. She was taller than most dancers but walked with the same posture: back straight, shoulders back, and chin held high.

Marina didn't go to Suitland, but a lot of Suitland students knew her because they had gone to the same junior high school. She was a cheerleader, very attractive, and very poised. Her mother was from Czechoslovakia but grew up in the southern part of Germany near the Czech-German border, and her father was Black. Through her mother's influence, Marina spoke German fluently.

Through the grapevine, I knew that during junior high Marina had dated a basketball player named Jimmy Williams, who was equally popular at the same school. Jimmy was tall and athletically talented and was projected to play in college or even professionally. For whatever reason, Jimmy and Marina had parted ways after junior high school. Jimmy was recruited for his basketball potential and went to high school at a private prep academy in nearby Oxon Hill—the same school, I believe, later attended by Kevin Durant, one of the all-time greats of professional basketball. Marina moved to a place seemingly remote from Suitland, both geographically and culturally, and enrolled at Paint Branch High School, where she excelled in both cheerleading and modern dance.

I knew Jimmy from playground ball, and we were even friends. I wanted to meet Marina but also wanted to be respectful of Jimmy in case he still had feelings for her. Ultimately, he was the one to introduce us, though only in passing and through chance when we ran into her at some event.

Shortly after our brief introduction, I saw Marina again at a basketball tournament in Montgomery County. I wanted to go over to her but was a bit shy because I wasn't sure that she would remember me and I didn't want to chance chumping myself. Besides, she was surrounded by a bunch of people. As I turned to go to the locker room, she gestured to me and walked over. We spoke for a few minutes, mainly about things going on at Suitland, but I needed to join my team in the locker room. She suggested that I call her to continue the conversation and jotted her phone number on a scrap of paper. It was weeks before I overcame my nervousness and finally called.

Not being one for small talk, I rarely stayed on the phone for more than a few seconds. I didn't enjoy phone conversations and was even anxious about them because I never knew what to say to keep the conversation going. I sensed that this might be the start of something special when the initial phone conversation with Marina lasted over an hour. The only reason I finally cut it off was that I was already late for a basketball game. Otherwise, I'm sure we would have stayed on the phone for another hour.

Marina reassured me that she and Jimmy really had broken up and that she had no interest in getting back together. There was another problem, though: she was seeing an older guy named Armando. After a few more phone calls, the sparks flying between us were undeniable, and she broke up with him.

I don't recall our conversations, but we did have a few things in common. We both were biracial with Black military fathers and were light-skinned but self-identified strongly as Black. And because she went to junior high school with people who now went to Suitland High with me, our circle of friends and acquaintances overlapped.

We started dating, and being with Marina changed my focus. I stopped party-hopping with Eddie and stopped seeing Debbie. I still worked, but otherwise it was basketball, schoolwork, and Marina.

We saw each other practically every weekend. Sometimes we would go out and sometimes she would come over to my family's Shady Grove apartment, but usually I would go over to her house. She lived about forty-five minutes away when traffic was good on the 405 freeway, but typically the commute would take well over an hour. Occasionally, we would have a snowstorm that made travel very difficult and hazardous. It didn't matter. I would put chains on the tires and slowly make my way up the freeway to see her.

I loved going over to her house and spending time not only with her but with her family. Her mother, Ernestine, was a stay-at-home mom and the nucleus of the family. The first time I met her, I brought over some strong German beer for her. I didn't know it at the time, but it was a hard-to-find brand and was her favorite. I was in with her after that initial introduction.

Marina's father, Tony, had served in the military—and met Ernestine when he was on duty in Germany. He retired from the military but continued to work for the government in a civilian capacity. He had really liked Jimmy because he thought Jimmy was going to be a professional basketball player and make a lot of money. He ended up liking me also because he thought I was smart and was going to be a successful doctor.

Tony was very conscious of social status. He had intended to move the family out of Prince George County to Montgomery County because it was a more prestigious address. To this day, Montgomery County is one of the wealthiest counties in the United States. He was very disappointed when he found out that his street was on the dividing line between the counties of Prince George and Montgomery, and that his house was on the Prince George County side.

Marina had six siblings: Kenny, Rodney, Dwight, Craig, Vicky, and Jules. Unlike my relationship with Dianna at the time, the siblings were close to each other, and I got to know each well. It was the type of family unit I had not witnessed except on television, and I felt a part of it. Days that previously held no meaning for me were now special, especially Christmas, but also Thanksgiving as well as birthdays. For Christmas, I helped get the tree and decorate it and exchanged presents; on Thanksgiving, I ate as part of the family; birthdays were always recognized with cards and gifts and celebrated with special dinners.

It was the perfect family life. They had a nice house that was almost in Montgomery County, Marina and her siblings all went to well-funded suburban schools, their dad drove the latest model Lincoln Continental Mark III, and their mom tended to everyone's needs with love and affection. I realize now that they were not rich, but they were the most solidly middle-class family I knew. I remember being introduced to filet mignon at a family dinner once. The steak was so good I had two or three helpings. It was only later that I found out how expensive these cuts of steak were. No one had made me feel that I was being greedy or that I was unwelcome at the dinner table.

Perhaps the greatest gift I received from Marina and her family was their belief in me. They made me feel that I was smart and talented, and that I would enjoy extraordinary success in life. I'm not sure on what basis they had made this assessment. I had good grades, but I was just in high school. For whatever reason, they constantly communicated their high hopes for me, which had a profound effect on my confidence. At the time, I was not even considering medical school, but Marina's parents often mentioned that I would be a physician. Their belief in me had an impact.

I initially could not believe that such a sophisticated, popular girl like Marina was my girlfriend. She treated me as if I was the one who was special and that she was the one who was fortunate and lucky. Things were great for the most part, but like many high school relationships, there were a few ups and downs. Marina's oldest brother, Kenny, had a girlfriend, Lynn, who went to McKinley High School in Washington, D.C. After I had dated Marina for about nine months, at the end of our junior year Lynn invited Marina and me to go to her high school prom with Kenny and her. I had a test I needed to study for and declined the invitation. Marina went and Lynn introduced her to a street guy named Angelo. Like Eddie, my friend from Shady Grove apartments, he was one of these cool popular guys who no longer went to high school—I'm not sure if he had graduated or had dropped out—but everyone in school still knew him.

Marina was smitten. Angelo called her "stuff" as a term of endearment. She thought that was cool and began calling her toddler brother, Jules, "stuff." All the signs were there. She was enamored with Angelo and I knew it. I could have tried to keep her and would probably have been successful. But I didn't want to risk being dumped, so I broke up with her. I was very macho about it and didn't want to show that I was hurt. *I did not need anyone!* She was very conflicted—wanting us to stay together but being drawn to this new experience—and cried. After I broke up with her, she started dating Angelo.

During the time that Marina was dating Angelo, I went to visit her brother Craig, who was having a neurosurgical procedure performed at the Walter Reed National Military Medical Center. As I was getting off an elevator, Angelo was waiting to get in. As sometimes occurs with men who are competing for something, we sized each other up and made a mental calculation as to whether we could take the other physically if necessary. *I could, no doubt*, I thought. We exchanged nods and that was it.

The relationship with Angelo was short-lived. After several months of dating him, Marina wanted us to get back together. I guess the novelty of going out with a "cool" D.C. street guy had worn off. Although I wasn't seeing anyone special, I was going out and dating other girls. But I had stayed in touch with Marina's family, particularly her mother, and occasionally went to their home to visit. Marina and I started spending time together on these visits and eventually we became a couple again, much to the delight of her parents. But I lost a little something with the experience—blind trust, youthful innocence—and became a bit wary of showing my vulnerability with her, or with anyone else.

One day, about a year later, we went to the mall and I went into a shoe store to get a pair of basketball shoes. As I was trying them on, the clerk kneeling at my feet looked up and our eyes locked. It was Angelo. He completed the fitting, and I paid for the shoes and walked out. Marina met me at the door. She didn't show any signs of being aware of what had just happened, and I didn't say anything.

I later found out that Lynn hadn't liked me for some reason and had orchestrated Marina meeting Angelo. She was very status conscious and had broken up with Kenny to go out with a guy who was pre-med at Colby College in Waterville, Maine. Kenny had a good government job, but Lynn wanted to be a doctor's wife. She and the pre-med student never married.

When I was at Harvard Medical School, I did a month rotation at Howard University's medical school. One day, I walked into the hospital and asked the information receptionist for directions. It was Lynn. She looked a bit embarrassed, and I understood why. She had tried to undermine a good relationship for some groundless reason, and here I was, a Harvard doctor.

∽∽

I went to Allegheny College, a small liberal arts school in Meadville, Pennsylvania. Marina was looking at a different set of colleges. Although there was never an explicit plan to stay together—at least that I was aware of—she ended up going to Edinboro State College in Edinboro, Pennsylvania, a forty-five-minute drive north from Meadville. The arrangement was fine with me: she was close enough that we could see each other occasionally but not so close as to become a distraction.

I was very committed to my studies and planned to work hard. I knew that I was probably not as academically prepared as most of the other kids at Allegheny who went to more rigorous high schools and I would need to make up for it by studying longer and being more focused. If I did not do as well as some of my colleagues, it was not going to be because I was outworked. I shunned fraternities, getting drunk, or even socializing much. I had a girlfriend who was just forty-five minutes away, so all of my time at Allegheny was going to be committed to studying and basketball.

Soon all of that would change. Allegheny's third game of the 1972–73 season was on December 6 at Edinboro. Prior to the game, before I joined the other players in the locker room, Marina introduced me to several of her college friends. One of them was Edinboro's star football running back. There was a certain nervousness in her behavior around him and I suspected something. After the game, I had a bit of time because the junior varsity team was playing. I went to her dorm room, and her football friend came by to drop off a load of clothes for her to wash. I was no dummy—who does laundry for a friend?

I didn't say anything then but went back to Edinboro the following week to break up with her. Wanting us to stay together, she applied to Allegheny as a transfer student and was surprised when they enthusiastically accepted her. It really should not have been a surprise: she graduated in the top quarter of her class in a very good high school, had a solid B+ grade average, and had impressive extracurricular activities including cheerleading and modern dance, and she was Black at a time when Black students were being actively recruited by liberal arts colleges. At any rate, she started at Allegheny after the first Christmas holiday break, and we spent the next three and a half years together.

Although it had not been planned, Marina's transfer to Allegheny was a net positive. Allegheny was a small school in a small town. There was not a lot to do socially, and having a girlfriend who lived in the same dormitory filled what could have become a lonely void. However, the experience also exposed basic differences in our worldviews and approaches to life.

One such incident occurred during finals week. I had worked tirelessly, studying and completing my assignments. Marina, on the other hand, had taken a more lackadaisical approach. As the deadline for a finals paper approached, it was obvious that she was not going to be able to complete it without substantial assistance from other classmates, including me, and that's what we did.

Afterward, I was upset with Marina and spoke to one of our faculty friends, Mr. Bickerstaff, about it. I told him I'd worked hard and believed that she should have also, rather than rely on the assistance of others. What if we had not come to her rescue? His response surprised me, and I've thought about it often since that time. Rather than agreeing with me on the importance of hard work and self-reliance, he replied that Marina was attractive and likable and that people were going to respond to her in that way. Further, he explained, she knew it and counted on it. It had become part of her approach to life.

I thought Mr. Bickerstaff was probably right, but only to a certain extent. People reacted to Marina in a certain way now, in part, because she was young and attractive. As with everyone, she was going to age and the way people perceived her beauty would diminish. At some point, she would be forced to rely less on superficial attributes and have to draw deeply into a reservoir of knowledge, skills, and work ethic. These more foundational attributes would likely be insufficiently developed as she would not have put in the grueling work to cultivate them. As Mr. Bickerstaff keenly observed, she didn't have a need to do so.

Marina received a surprise gift of a new Camaro from her parents for graduation. It was parked right outside her dorm with a big ribbon and bow around it. We decided to drive it down to Maryland and stop in Pittsburgh to visit my roommate from my freshman year, Jesse, a basketball player who had left Allegheny when he became academically ineligible to play. Jesse lived with his parents in a housing project, and they welcomed us to stay the night so that we could attend a big citywide high school basketball tournament that evening. Marina was uncomfortable with the neighborhood, which could accurately be characterized as "the hood," and wanted to continue traveling. But many of the basketball courts I played on and house parties I went to during high school were in the hood, so it was not a big deal for me, and I really wanted to see the basketball tournament. I shamed her as being too "uppity" and got my way. When we got up the next morning to get on the road, we couldn't find the car—it had been stolen, right in front of Jesse's apartment building!

I don't remember exactly what happened next, but the police were involved and the car was recovered within hours. It had been taken for a joyride and dropped off on a side street. There was some greasy chicken and french fries left on the seats, but the car was otherwise in perfect condition. I felt foolish for insisting that we stay overnight despite Marina's apprehension and knew we had lucked out. We completed our drive home to Maryland in silence.

After Allegheny, Marina went to Cleveland to get a master's degree in education, and I went to Boston for medical school. We kept in touch and had an on-again, off-again relationship for years afterward. Our relationship didn't end with a bang; it just kind of petered out. Many years after high school, Marina wanted to surprise me with a party to which she planned to invite all of my former basketball teammates and other friends from high school. When I learned of her plans, I asked that she cancel them. Those were high school days, and I believed in looking forward, never backward.

One of the novels I enjoyed reading in high school was *Rabbit, Run*, part of the Rabbit series by John Updike. The protagonist, Harry Angstrom, a former high school basketball star, can't quite adjust to life without stardom and is stuck in a dead-end job and a loveless marriage. The book follows his attempts to escape the constraints of his life. Reading this as a cautionary tale, I resolved to always look to the future and continue to develop and evolve—throughout life. Although I appreciated the thought behind Marina's attempted party, my identity was branching out in so many new ways; my glory days as a high school basketball star were great at the time but I had no desire to relive them. It was the same with our relationship. We had changed, and the only thing that drew us sporadically back together was our shared past.

George Webber, the protagonist of Thomas Wolfe's novel *You Can't Go Home Again*, realizes at the end of the novel: *"You can't go . . . back home to your childhood . . . back home to a young man's dreams of glory and of fame . . . back home . . . to the old forms and systems of things which once seemed everlasting but which are changing all the time—back home to the escapes of time and Memory."* Eventually, I needed to move on—from high school and from Marina.

9

Ms. Stephan

When I first entered Ms. Judy Stephan's English classroom, I had no idea that she would change my life. In fact, her impact on my life trajectory—choice of college, ability to think critically and communicate effectively, development of social consciousness, appreciation of the arts—is incalculable.

Suitland is a big school and I had not met her prior to my first day of eleventh-grade English class. Ms. Stephan sat behind a big desk so all I could see was her upper body. Halfway through class, she planted both arms firmly on the desk and rose slowly from her chair. It seemed like it was a struggle for her to do so, as if she were pushing herself up with the strength of her arms. Once up, she steadied herself with one arm still on the desk, and with the other arm she grabbed two metal forearm crutches from behind her. Then she started walking to the center of the room, first firmly and deliberately planting her left leg and then swinging her right leg as if the entire motion was being initiated from the hip. It was clear her right leg was just dead weight.

I later found out that Ms. Stephan was disabled from polio. She probably contracted it in the late 1940s when the virus was at its peak, before the widespread vaccinations of the mid-1950s. Ms. Stephan often quipped that she was born a little too early.

In spite of her paralysis, Ms. Stephan was completely self-reliant. She had extraordinary arm strength and was able to walk long distances with the help of her crutches. She even drove a car that was equipped with a special contraption that allowed her to control everything, including the brakes and gas pedal, by hand.

I wasn't sure what to make of her initially; first impressions can be deceiving. I would come to understand that what defined Ms. Stephan was not her crutches but her extraordinary will, resilience, and power of conviction.

Two years later, before I left for college, Ms. Stephan recounted her impressions of me when I first entered her classroom. As someone with a physical handicap, she valued brains over brawn and harbored a bias against athletes. "Oh no, a dumb jock in my classroom," she had thought to herself as I leisurely shuffled into the room and took a seat in the back. She reflected later that I was the most eager-to-learn student she had encountered and that I sparked a renewed sense of purpose in her as a teacher.

Ms. Stephan's English class was during the fourth period, the period directly after lunch, and I often fell asleep during class. This was before I was dating Marina, when I was still running the streets at night or working in addition to playing basketball every day. She confronted me about it one day when all the other students had departed the class and I was still there with my head resting on the desk. "I'm not going to allow you to fall asleep in my class!" she shouted. "Either you stay up and pay attention or get out of my class." I was not completely forthright in my reply when I told her that I was sleepy because I had to work nights; that was only partially true. Thankfully she had some sympathy for me, and by the following week, we worked out an arrangement that accommodated my need to rest and her need to fulfill her responsibilities as my teacher. By then, she had recognized that I was getting all As on my assignments and that I was not being challenged academically. She allowed me to skip her class so that I could go to the gym locker room and sleep on one of the benches. Since lunch break was directly before her class, it was possible for me to get about ninety minutes of uninterrupted naptime. In return, I had to commit to extra reading and writing assignments that I could complete on my own time.

As the semester progressed, the assignments became increasingly difficult and she kept a tight rein on my progress through weekly assignment review meetings. Under her guidance, I read the novels of Kurt Vonnegut, Somerset

Maugham, Ken Kesey, Ernest Hemingway, William Faulkner, Ayn Rand, and Fyodor Dostoevsky among many others as well as nonfiction works by Charles Darwin, Jean-Paul Sartre, and Henry David Thoreau. Fortunately, I was a fast reader and was able to keep up with everything she threw at me.

One of the most impactful books I read during this time was *Passions of the Mind*, a biographical novel by Irving Stone about Sigmund Freud. It was not one of Ms. Stephan's selections; I chose it on my own, though I probably wouldn't have picked it up had she not encouraged my literary awareness. After reading this book, I became fascinated by Freudian theory and proceeded to read many of his most influential books, including *The Interpretation of Dreams*, *The Ego and the Id*, and *The Psychopathology of Everyday Life* as well as books on analytical psychology by Carl Jung. For the first time, I started imagining a career that didn't involve athletics. I could be a psychoanalyst, a thought that became the driving force behind my desire to go to college.

While I enjoyed discussing literature with Ms. Stephan, I was especially captivated by our talks about evolution and existential philosophy. We also had many discussions about my role in society and my obligation to do something to positively impact the world. Her expectations for me were high, but she also thought that I needed guidance to avoid pitfalls and to achieve what she perceived to be my potential.

Much of her caution and skepticism was born out of experience. As a woman with a physical handicap, she often described the discrimination she had faced when she interviewed for certain corporate positions. She talked of men much less capable or of shallow but attractive women being selected over her. She warned me of the discrimination and racism I would face as a Black man. She warned me that I would have to work a lot harder—and would have to perform a lot better—than others if I were to have a chance at fair consideration. It was a message reminiscent of G.O.'s back in Misawa, and I listened.

Ms. Stephan went above and beyond the call of duty. She continued to guide and tutor me after I had completed her class. Near the end of my senior year, I was getting anxious about the senior prom. The students planning the prom were coming up with extravagant, and what I would later recognize as outlandish, ideas for the venue, such as the White House, and all of the plans included a formal dinner. I had never experienced formal dining and was concerned that I might unknowingly violate proper etiquette. I confided my anxiety to Ms. Stephan.

She told me not to worry and that she would teach me. I assumed this meant we would take a few minutes during one of our review sessions to go over which utensils to use with which course. Several weeks later, Ms. Stephan surprised me. "We have reservations this Friday at one of my favorite French restaurants, La Niçoise, in Georgetown," she causally informed me in a matter-of-fact tone. "Wear a tie, and be ready for me to pick you up at your apartment at 7:00 sharp."

The best restaurants in Washington, D.C., at the time were French. La Niçoise was carefully selected by Ms. Stephan because it wasn't as formal as some of them but still very good. It had a unique flair in that the waiters, wearing tuxedos, all zipped around on roller skates. I still remember the dinner. It was classic French: we started with escargot, had a main course of chateaubriand, and ended with chocolate mousse. What I remember even more than the food is the wine. The drinking age at the time was eighteen, and I was close enough. It was a Louis Jadot Pommard from the Cote de Beaune of Burgundy. I took one drink of the Pommard with a bite of the chateaubriand and had an epiphany. So, this was what wine was supposed to taste like! Up to then, I had only had Boone's Farm, Ripple, or Thunderbird, and the Pommard was from a different world.

In the end, the prom dinner was a letdown. It was held in the ballroom of a lower-end hotel chain, and my newfound dining etiquette was not even put to the test. La Niçoise was nonetheless a life-altering experience. Before we graduated, I took Marina there to make up for the disappointing hotel prom dinner, and we had a terrific time. Since then, I've dined at many of Washington's fine French restaurants—Sans Souci, Maison Blanche, Jean-Pierre, Rive Gauche—and in truth most of them were better than La Niçoise. Yet, because of that experience, when Ms. Stephan introduced me to fine leisure dining with good French wine, La Niçoise remained one of my very favorite places to dine in Washington until it finally closed in the 1990s.

Ms. Stephan opened me to a world of culture I had not known; it was the beginning of my understanding and appreciation of life's aesthetic joys. Ms. Stephan was remarkably active, and one of her favorite pastimes was to go to the Kennedy Center for the Performing Arts to enjoy theater, dance, and music. Her eyes would light up when she described these performances to me. Many years later, as president of Wayne State University, I had the opportunity to watch its dance troupe perform at the Kennedy Center, and I thought about Ms. Stephan and how she had introduced me to this magnificent venue. Her passion for supporting the performing arts has had a lasting effect on my own views. I believe that the performing arts are the soul of culturally vibrant communities, and one of my proudest accomplishments has been building Wayne State's $65 million performing arts center. Called the Hilberry Gateway Project, in recognition of Wayne State's fourth president, it serves symbolically as the entry to the heart of Wayne State's physical campus.

Of the many governing boards on which I've served, one of the most satisfying has been that of the Detroit Symphony Orchestra (DSO). The DSO, along with the Detroit Institute of Arts, is a cultural anchor of midtown Detroit. Wayne State University sits within blocks of both and is nourished by their presence. As Julie Garwood, the author of multiple *New York Times* best-selling books, once remarked, "Education isn't just about feeding the brain. Art and music feed the heart and soul."

Early in my senior year, Ms. Stephan asked me about college. My plan had been to go to college on an athletic scholarship—I had already received recruitment interest for basketball from several scouts—but I had not given much thought to which college I'd choose or even what type. When I mentioned one name of a college that had expressed interest in recruiting me off the top of my head, I saw a fleeting frown come across her face. "Are you sure that's the type of place you want to go to?" she probed. I had no idea if it was or not.

My official guidance counselor was not much help. We had over two thousand students at Suitland and I don't actually remember ever meeting her. My best friend, Michael Everett, got a scholarship to play football at Florida A&M. A few others received athletic scholarships to attend one of the local community colleges or regional colleges. These were the exceptions, though. Most of the students I knew, athletes or not, were not planning to go to college, so it wasn't a topic I knew a lot about.

Ms. Stephan, on the other hand, had some strong beliefs on the subject, and she didn't hesitate to make her thoughts known. She wanted me to aim high and to prioritize academics over athletics. She also believed that I should go to a small liberal arts school in a small-town community far from Washington, D.C. High on her list were Marietta and Oberlin, and I went to Ohio to visit both. But I was most intrigued with Allegheny College because the basketball coach there had been recruiting me, and it also happened to meet with Ms. Stephan's approval. When the coach came up with a financial package that allowed me to go to college without out-of-pocket expenses, it sealed the deal.

With about eighteen hundred students, Allegheny was smaller than my high school and there weren't many Black students. The only other Black player on the basketball team was Jesse, a 6'7" freshman forward from Pittsburgh. Unsurprisingly, we were paired together as roommates, but that wouldn't last for long. Allegheny used a trimester system with three courses per trimester comprising a full load. Jesse failed math that first trimester and could not play basketball. After another trimester or two, he dropped out of school altogether.

Jesse was bright and I am convinced that he would have successfully graduated had he been able to pass that first math course. I later discovered, as a college administrator, that introductory college math is considered a "barrier" course, one of the courses that impede progress to degree completion for many students in their first year. As a result, I have advocated for greater flexibility in the requirement of traditional math as part of a college core curriculum. For example, I believe that statistics is a more valuable discipline to learn than traditional math for many students and that it should be accepted as a substitute in the core curriculum.

Math was certainly a barrier, but it was more than that. Jesse did not feel supported by the team or the college. He had gone to an urban high school, Pittsburgh

Fifth Avenue, where he was the leading scorer. Like me, he had a strong bond with his high school teammates, and he was lonely without them. I am convinced that he would have persevered, stayed in school, and played basketball after the following semester had he felt more supported by his Allegheny teammates.

⁓

College was a huge adjustment for me and started off being very difficult. The workload was enormous and I felt overwhelmed. If I wasn't playing basketball, I was in my dorm room, alone, studying late into the night. I was one of only three freshmen to make the varsity basketball team and that added an additional load on my schedule. Neither of my parents had gone to college so I couldn't turn to them for advice. I was just lost.

During orientation, all freshmen students had been given a placement exam to determine eligibility to take English 1. The exam was primarily to determine level of writing ability. I was the only Black freshman student to pass. Everyone else was placed in remedial English or introductory English. That didn't make me feel overly confident, but I wasn't surprised either. I thought I was a good writer. But at the midpoint of the first trimester, my progress report showed that I had two Bs and a C, and the C was in English 1.

My first major writing assignment in English 1 was an analysis of a book, the title of which I no longer remember. What I do remember is that the review was returned with a lot of red ink and a C– on the top. I learned later that the professor, Dr. Frank, was a very hard grader and that a C– was not that bad. At the time, though, I was devastated.

I called Ms. Stephan. At my request, she reviewed the written assignment and while she agreed that the grading was harsh, she did not think that it was unfair. I remember her commenting that "it was okay for high school but not for college" and going through every redlined item with me to explain how it could have been written better. She went even further. She called Professor Frank and spoke to him. I don't know what they discussed, but his attitude toward me seemed to change after the call. The next writing assignment was a critique of Amiri Baraka's *Preface to a Twenty Volume Suicide Note*. I received an A, a rarity in Dr. Frank's class.

That was a turning point for college. I salvaged the first trimester—I believe I ended up with an A and two Bs—and never looked back. Four years later, I graduated magna cum laude with a GPA just shy of 3.9 (out of 4.0).

The A that first trimester was in Psychology 1. I did well but did not enjoy the class. The class had a very heavy behavioral psychology skew, but I believed that behaviorism was shallow. Having been enthralled with Freud and Jung in high school, my interest was more in the deeper analyses of the mind. My career interest was to become a psychoanalyst and my plan was to get a Ph.D. in psychology. Since Allegheny was a small college and the psychology department did not have professors who taught classical psychoanalysis, Ms. Stephan suggested that I get a medical degree instead and approach psychoanalysis through psychiatry. Since eleventh grade, Ms. Stephan had subtly encouraged me to become a doctor. I later found out that she had approved of Allegheny as my college choice because of its outstanding record of sending graduates to medical school. I would end up pursuing medicine as my career, as she had hoped all along.

During a break in my first semester of medical school, I attempted to take Ms. Stephan to lunch to thank her for guiding me into medicine. On the way to the restaurant, we drove down Pennsylvania Avenue in downtown Washington. As we took a turn on Constitution Avenue, we noticed a huge crowd of people waiting to get into a building. The line was blocks long. Curious, we drove around the block to get a better look. The building was the National Gallery of Art, and the King Tut exhibition was premiering. Ms. Stephan suggested that we skip lunch and check it out. We parked and waited in line for more than three hours to get in.

I love museums and have visited the great ones in most of the major cities around the world. Some, like the Louvre in Paris, I've visited many times. But my first museum experience was the blockbuster exhibition *Treasures of Tutankhamun* with Ms. Stephan.

Although I benefited more from our friendship than she did, it wasn't totally one-sided. I remember visiting her at Suitland one afternoon toward the end of the school day when I was home from medical school. Despite the passing of five or six years since I graduated, I immediately felt a deep sense of comfort and familiarity when I entered her classroom. Ms. Stephan was excited to see me, but I had dropped by unannounced and she seemed to be in a bit of a hurry to get somewhere. I was stunned to discover that she was going to watch a Suitland basketball game and she didn't want to be late—not even for me. *Seriously? A basketball game?*

It turns out that Ms. Stephan, who previously shunned athletes and was openly dismayed when I walked into her class years earlier, was now the basketball team's biggest fan. She invited me to go with her. When we walked into the gym, all of the Suitland players stopped what they were doing to acknowledge her. She knew every single player by name. I thought it ironically humorous that I had been a star basketball player, the team captain at Suitland, and none of the players even recognized me; Ms. Stephan had detested basketball players and all the players knew and were fond of her.

When I graduated from high school, Ms. Stephan gave me a present: *The World Atlas of Wine* by Hugh Johnson. Now in its eighth edition, it was first published in 1971 and has been recognized as the most essential and authoritative wine reference available. I glanced through it occasionally, but it wasn't until after I had completed my ophthalmology and glaucoma training that I took the opportunity to thoroughly read it, cover to cover, remembering that first sip of Pommard. By that time, 1986 or so, I had some discretionary income, so I began to study and collect wine. My interest hasn't waned. I wouldn't claim to be at the level of a sommelier, but I'm fairly knowledgeable and keep a good collection of about fifteen hundred bottles or so in a private cellar. Some of my most valuable are Bordeaux wines that I bought in the 1980s, and I enjoy sharing them with special friends.

Throughout my last two years of college, I took courses in subjects that expanded my horizons—art, classical music, philosophy, mythology, and literature—and took trips to art museums and symphony concerts in Pittsburgh and Cleveland. I felt freedom to do so rather than take the usual pre-med science curriculum because of my belief that I had secured a spot in medical school a year early. Ms. Stephan would always comment that I was like a sponge, soaking up whatever knowledge I could. That thirst for knowledge would endure well after college and persists today.

Ms. Stephan had limited opportunities to travel abroad, but she would often implore me to explore the world. The courses I took during my last year of college whetted my appetite, and I resolved to experience the museums, the symphonies, and the operas in all the major cultural centers of Europe and Asia. I've been fortunate enough to fulfill much of that quest and have been able to expose my two kids, Yoshio and Presley, to the cultural wonders of the world as well. But it was Ms. Stephan who started me on this journey of lifelong learning, and my life has been so enriched by it.

One day in the early 1990s when I was seeing patients at the Jules Stein Eye Institute of UCLA, I received a surprise call from her. She wanted to let me know that the physical demands of teaching with polio had become overwhelming and that she was retiring and moving to Lexington, Kentucky, where her brother lived. I hadn't spoken to her for decades at that point, so I was moved when she informed me that she had been keeping up with my successes and was proud of me. I was also overwhelmed with emotion as I reminisced about our time together in high school and her impact on my personal and academic growth. Although I understood her rationale for retiring, I was so sad that Ms. Stephan would no longer be teaching high school.

In 2009 or so, I had a work-related reason to visit the University of Kentucky in Lexington so I decided to visit her. We hadn't seen each other since the time I visited her during medical school when she took me to Suitland's basketball game. I didn't know what to expect. She was in a wheelchair now, but other than that, she was the same Ms. Stephan I remembered from high school. Although she had retired from full-time teaching, she was doing some academic tutoring for members of the Kentucky basketball team. She mentioned Rajon Rondo and John Wall—both of whom were all-stars in the pros—as former students.

That night I took her to dinner. I had researched the local restaurants prior to my arrival and found one that was handicap accessible and well regarded. I also preordered a special bottle of wine—a Pommard from Louis Jadot.

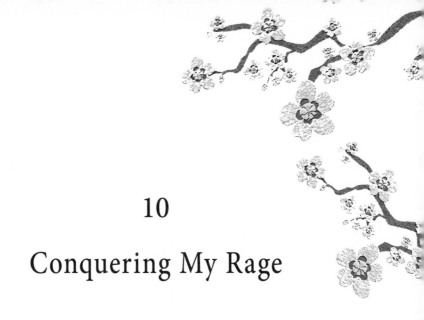

10

Conquering My Rage

Throughout my childhood and adolescence, I fought a lot. Usually the reason for a fight fell into one of three categories: (1) someone said something about my mother, (2) someone was bullying a weaker person who couldn't fight back, or (3) someone teased me about my stuttering. Yes, I was a stutterer, and I stuttered a lot.

Fortunately, I won most of my fights. I think I was probably a good fighter because I had an extreme temper and would go all out in a rage without regard for my own safety. Once I committed to a fight, I felt no sense of hesitation.

All of that started to change after a near altercation that took place when I was a young faculty physician in Los Angeles. I was playing in a pick-up basketball game on Venice Beach when I got into an argument with an opposing player. I had seen the other guy around the court but I didn't know him. He wore baggy jeans, no shirt, and, oddly, given the context, a heavy chain around his neck. He was athletic but had no discipline. Both his erratic behavior and irritating mouthing off suggested that he was on drugs, amphetamines or some other type of uppers. At one point, he undercut me as I was going up for what should have been an easy uncontested layup. Fouls can be hard in playground ball, and that's just part of the game, but the one thing you don't do is undercut someone. I went after him and we went chest to chest. But before any punches were thrown, teammates from both sides interceded and separated us.

An acquaintance of mine from Boston, who was visiting Los Angeles and witnessed the altercation, took me aside and with a tone of disbelief, exhorted, "What the hell are you thinking? You have everything to lose and this guy has nothing to lose. You stupid or something?"

He was right. At that point in my life, I was a glaucoma specialist who performed eye surgery. The other guy was from the streets and probably didn't even have a job. I could have lost my livelihood if I broke my hand on the guy's face—my friend joked that his face was ugly and it would not have even mattered if it got all messed up. I don't think I've been in a real fight since I came to that realization.

Growing up, I was really good at judo and progressed in the ranks at an accelerated pace. As I became more expert, I was confident that no one could beat me. Interestingly, though, the more I progressed in the ranks, the less I fought in the streets. Part of my restraint might have been due to the fact that I was getting older and more mature. The primary reason, though, was that I had become enamored with the general philosophy of the martial arts, with a particular interest in the philosophical foundation that undergirded the great shaolin priests of China and samurais of Japan. Key among their virtues was self-control, and I resolved to improve upon, if not master, my own. This would prove to be a lifelong journey.

I have a long way to go but I am still learning from their example and practicing better self-control. In fact, people now often remark on my equanimity, even in the face of extreme provocation. But family members and close friends from my younger days have seen a different side of me.

Even after I stopped fighting, I was prone to road rage. When I was a first-year medical student, I was coming out of the parking lot at Vanderbilt Hall, the residence for Harvard medical students, when a car abruptly cut me off. Even more infuriating, the driver gave me the finger. I tailed him through the Harvard medical complex but he didn't get very far because of heavy traffic on Longwood Boulevard, the main street that ran through it. When his car was stopped, I jumped out in the middle of traffic and tapped on his window, which he rolled down, apparently not expecting what would happen next. Without uttering a word, I punched him in the face. I still remember his glasses being skewed on his face—I probably broke them—and blood coming from his nose as I turned around and got back into my car.

My road rage was extreme, and I repeatedly put every member of my family, as well as many friends, at risk of an accident, or retaliation from whoever was in the other car. I was fortunate that I never encountered a person with a gun.

But that didn't preclude me from embarrassment. One time when I was cut off, I followed the offending car, aggressively honking my horn. The car was barely chugging along as I pulled alongside it to stare down the driver. I was never more chastened than when I looked over and saw an eighty-year-old woman struggling with her sight and reflexes. She was one of my patients.

Seeing this elderly lady who was a widower and lived alone, and who I knew to have compromised vision, struggling to drive and maintain some level of independence was a shameful moment for me. More than the threat of being hurt by a deranged person with a gun, this incident made me realize that I had to control my road rage. To this day, I do not know if she recognized the rude person honking at her as her ophthalmologist.

Unfortunately, my episodes of rage weren't confined to the road. One time when I was an ophthalmology resident and living on Beacon Hill in Boston, I stopped by a local sandwich shop after work, tired and hungry, and ordered a steak and cheese sub, no onions or mayo. One thing to know about me is that I absolutely hate mayonnaise. The young man behind the grill was flirting with some girl and not being particularly attentive to me. When I got my sub, it had mayo on it. Initially, I didn't lose my temper and asked him to remake the sandwich. Instead of doing so, he scraped the mayo off the bun and tried to give it back to me. I yelled, "I told you no mayo!" reached across the counter, and punched him in the face. He came around the counter and connected with a roundhouse right to my left eye. Momentarily dazed, I grabbed him and we grappled with each other while the girl he'd been flirting with screamed and cried. I don't remember how the fight was stopped, but I do know that the manager of the place got involved and the guy lost his job. I also know that my vision was blurry and I had to go to the emergency room of the Mass Eye and Ear Infirmary, where I was training, for medical attention. This unfortunate incident, all because I didn't want mayo on my sandwich, eventually led to a surprising diagnosis that I'll reveal later.

As I got older, many of my altercations did not result in a fight but they were altercations nonetheless. A particularly consequential one took place when I was an intern in medicine at the Harlem Hospital Center. Late one night, I got into a dispute with the chief resident over how to treat a patient who was in a diabetic crisis. The argument devolved into me cursing and shouting at him and challenging him to a fight, an exchange that was witnessed by several nurses on the floor. As the chief resident walked away, one of the nurses grabbed my arm and asked, "What's wrong with you?"

The next morning, I was called into the office of the chair of medicine, Dr. Gerald E. Thompson, an imposing figure who was one of the only African Americans to reach the rank of full professor at Columbia's medical school. Because of his initials, "G.E.T.," everyone referred to him as the "JET." The JET was revered. Like EF Hutton, in its popular commercial, when the JET talked, people listened.

I'll never forget what he told me, as he sat in a big chair behind an imposing desk, while I sat across from him in what felt like a little kiddie chair. "Roy, you went against my chief resident, and that's like going against me. It doesn't matter who was right or wrong. As chief resident, he represents me and deserved respect. If you do something like this when you get back to Boston for your residency, those white people are going to kick you out of medicine. Some of them will be looking for an excuse to kick you out and you are going to give them that excuse. You have great potential, and an opportunity in Boston that few Blacks will ever have. I'm going to give you another chance. I believe in you, but you have to change as you may never again get another chance."

A couple of years later, I read a news clipping about one of my fellow interns who committed suicide after the JET kicked him out of his residency for cocaine use. I don't condone what the medical resident did, but this was 1984 and he certainly was not the only physician at Harlem Hospital who used cocaine. His infraction was arguably less egregious than what I had done, calling out the chief resident to fight. It made me wonder what I would have done if the JET had kicked me out.

Thankfully, I would never know. Instead that meeting was the beginning of my transformation in the way I approached conflict resolution. Several decades later, the JET and I shared a podium as speakers at a symposium. Figuratively, I had always looked up to him. I was surprised to realize that he was not an actual physical giant—he was an average-size man, about two or three inches shorter than me. With humility and respect, I thanked him for not kicking me out of his medical internship program when he had every right to do so. He remembered the incident. He didn't say anything but just gave me a knowing smile. He had made the right decision and I had validated his faith in me.

Another incident that I have trouble shaking off happened more recently, albeit more than fifteen years ago. My ex-wife Suzanne and I were at the annual meeting of the American Academy of Ophthalmology in New Orleans. We were staying at the Ritz-Carlton and were getting into the lower-level elevator. Two guys were ahead of us; I didn't notice but one of them was the rap star LL Cool J. As Suzanne and I were about to enter the elevator, the other guy, LL Cool J's bodyguard, reached out his hand, stopped us from entering, and requested that we take the next elevator. Stunned by this gesture, I didn't know how to react, and the door closed in our faces. By the time I recovered, the elevator was gone.

The first floor at Ritz-Carltons is typically an entry floor to the elevators that take guests to the lobby level. There, a separate set of elevators, which are usually located on the opposite side of the lobby, go up to the various guest floors. I hurriedly got on the next elevator and got a glimpse of LL Cool J getting into a lobby elevator. What was particularly irksome was that other guests got on with him. I ran as fast as I could across the lobby to the elevator as it was closing. I wasn't able to get in but I was close enough to call him a punk and challenge him to come out. Now it was LL Cool J and his bodyguard who were surprised. I still remember the quizzical looks on their faces.

I regret this incident for two reasons. First, the other guests on the elevator were well-heeled white people, and a Black man cursing and calling out another Black man is not an image I want them to have witnessed. Also, I have a history of lower back muscle spasms because of a slight disc protrusion. Every several years, I do something that aggravates the bulge. In my rush to reach LL Cool J before his elevator door closed, I slipped and aggravated my back. I was incapacitated for weeks afterward. Although she did not like the way we were treated, Suzanne thought that I had acted like a fool and deserved whatever pain I brought upon myself. Perhaps she's right.

11

Dianna

When we moved to Suitland, my sister, Dianna, had a much different experience than I did. In some respects, Dianna was a younger version of me. She was smart, but not only in an academic sense; she had survival skills and street smarts. After all, she was five years younger than me and had survived near abandonment in Japan. She had grown up fast. Though small and petite in stature, she seemed mature beyond her years. Thinking back, I don't recall her having friends her age; the few I knew of were considerably older.

Dianna had issues with Dad, but they were not dissimilar to the ones I had with him when I was younger. He was strict and unemotional, and as a young girl who looked different from everyone else in her school, Dianna needed more from him. While she looked Asian, people knew that she had a Black father, and schoolmates teased her on both counts. I learned later that she was often taunted with chants of "nigger chink." As a little girl in Misawa, Dianna often was embarrassed to have a Black father. By her teen years, she didn't care much what schoolkids would say or think. Dianna didn't consider them her peers, but like most teen girls she still needed her father's support and affection, and Dad wasn't capable of providing either.

All my friends were Black and being Black was a big part of my identity. I hate to admit it, but, honestly, I was sometimes embarrassed to have an Asian mother. I didn't realize how important it was back then—I just took it for granted—but I had the backing of friends, most of whom were athletes nobody wanted to mess with. No one had Dianna's back. She confided in me about some things, but not everything. At the time, I was not fully aware of the depth of her suffering.

Dianna encountered challenges in school that I didn't experience. Her performance in school was similar to mine, although I sensed that she didn't have to work as hard at it. Dianna was subjected to ongoing sexual abuse, primarily by male teachers, and to physical bullying by classmates. Unlike me, she didn't participate in athletics and other extracurricular activities, not because of a lack of interest but because it would have been a luxury, an unnecessary distraction from her primary focus of surviving. Each day was a struggle for Dianna. She pleaded with Dad to take her out of that school and enroll her in the nearby Catholic school. When the answer was repeatedly "no," she decided to take matters into her own hands and leave.

At age thirteen, Dianna dropped out of school and ran away. No one knew her whereabouts, but after a month or so she reached out and introduced me to her boyfriend, an older guy named Brian, with whom she was living.

They lived in a garden-style apartment, not unlike our Shady Grove apartment but smaller. I only saw the living room, and the furnishings were sparse: a couch, a couple of chairs, and a television set. We sat there awkwardly facing each other, me staring at Brian as I tried to size him up.

Based on their body language, I didn't get the sense that Brian had masterminded any of Dianna's actions or even that he was in control of the situation. He had completed high school and served in the U.S. Marine Corps. He seemed like a typical "white boy." But Dianna, though only thirteen, exhibited a strong resolve and independence of thought. She was clearly a willing partner, not a pawn being manipulated by a Svengali.

"We're getting married and moving to Oregon where Brian is from," Dianna finally confessed.

Assuming I had not heard her correctly, I asked, "You're going where?"

"Hermiston, Oregon, east of Portland," she responded.

I was floored. Caught off guard and trying not to overreact, I took a deep breath and blurted out the first thing that came to mind. "You know, Dianna,

Oregon is very white. Your kids might take on more of Dad's traits and they may inherit dark skin. Are you and Brian ready for that possibility?"

Looking back, I'm not sure why that thought came to mind. Because of my own identity, perhaps I had assumed Dianna would be with a Black man and her having a Black child would not be an issue. Or perhaps I had a flashback to my mom raising a Black child in Japan and the difficulties she encountered with intolerance and racism. Whatever the reason, that thought reflected my state of mind, which made what happened next even more earth-shattering.

Dianna and Brian exchanged a look. Then Brian answered, "We spoke to your mother last week and she thought we should know that Dianna is fully Japanese." Brian had a strange expression on his face. I couldn't tell if he was just nervous or if it was a smirk.

I tensed as I glared across the couch at him. Twice in one sitting, within the span of just five minutes, I received shocking news for which I was unprepared. My dad was not Dianna's biological father. Although Dianna looked Asian, I had never considered the possibility that she had a Japanese father. The fact that we weren't full siblings was difficult for me to process at that moment. She had always been my little sister, and I had been her big brother. When we had no one else to depend on, we had each other. I felt betrayed, not by her but by the entire situation, and I felt a break in our bond. Furthermore, though it's possible that I would have reacted similarly, I wished that I had received the information from Dianna or from Mom rather than a complete stranger.

I felt like punching Brian. Instead, I didn't budge. I just sat there, speechless.

Within weeks, Dianna and Brian moved to the state of Oregon. Dad did not know what had happened to Dianna, and I didn't tell him until much later. Dianna had resolved to leave, no matter what, and he would have tried to stop her. Two strong personalities would have clashed, and I couldn't see anything positive coming out of that confrontation. He had gotten the message that she was alive and well, but that was about it. My dad was heartbroken and distraught, and it pained me to see him so deeply affected. But I also felt that I could not break Dianna's trust in me and betray her.

Soon after the move, Dianna and Brian had a child, Daniel. From what I could tell from the limited contact I had with her, they seemed very happy. Mom and I eventually told Dad about Dianna, Brian, and Daniel. He was ecstatic when Dianna came to visit with Daniel. And with Daniel, he displayed a tenderness that neither Dianna nor I had ever witnessed growing up. It seemed that all was forgiven.

Daniel died when he was eighteen months old. The cause of death was declared to be sudden infant death syndrome (SIDS), but I had my doubts. Ninety percent of SIDS deaths occur within the first six months of birth and it's almost unheard of after one year of age. It was not until recently, during the writing of this memoir, that Dianna revealed to me the real cause of Daniel's death. One night when Brian and Dianna went out to celebrate Dianna's birthday, Danny's babysitter, Brian's sister, neglected him and left a space heater on in an enclosed space. Daniel's death was avoidable; he died of heat stress.

Although she and Brian later had another child, Krista, Daniel's death seemed like the beginning of a downward spiral for both of them. They were both young and neither had the maturity or coping skills to deal with such a devastating event. I can speculate that guilt may also have been a contributing factor. Eventually Dianna and Brian divorced and she moved to Seattle, Washington.

Knowing what I know now, I could have had Brian arrested for statutory rape. It was a different time, though, and behavioral norms were not as clearly defined as they are now. Besides, Dianna's tenuous relationship with Dad had caused her to run away, and I felt that she needed me to be supportive. I faced a difficult dilemma and did what I thought was in the best interest of my sister at the time. I often wonder, though, how her life would have turned out had she not run away and had graduated, at least from high school.

Dianna summoned all of her survival skills when she moved to Seattle after her divorce. She arrived in the city on a bus with one quarter in her pocket, no place to sleep, no job, and no clothes except what she was wearing. Within a week, she was employed at the most prestigious country club in Seattle. Surrounded by Seattle's elite society during the day, she returned every night to a shelter in the worst part of town.

Expecting to go to college, Dianna took and passed the General Education Development test as an alternative to the high school diploma. She went to community college for a while but thought it was a complete waste of time and quit. The courses weren't challenging, and, besides, she already had the kind of job that her classmates were aspiring to obtain after earning their degrees.

Dianna got married to a guy named Bob. I liked Bob. Unlike Brian, he grew up in an Italian family in a multicultural, ethnically diverse neighborhood. He had a steady job at Boeing and was very responsible, but he wore a ponytail and had an independent, carefree persona. At some point, Dianna moved to Shoreline, a community nine miles north of downtown Seattle. Dianna's daughter, Krista, married a nice guy named Rob, and two grandkids, Genevieve and Luca, were born. They lived near Dianna in Shoreline.

On the surface, it appeared that things were going in a positive direction for her, but Dianna was frequenting casinos and gambling. I don't know when it happened, but at some point, like with Mom, Dianna became addicted. In retrospect, it may have begun with the trauma of losing a child at such a young age. Growing up, I never thought I would witness someone else as addicted to gambling as my mom. I was wrong, and gambling has taken a huge toll on Dianna's life.

She initially played casino games for fun but developed a pathological interest in poker. She couldn't stop playing it, and she became a compulsive gambler.

Compulsive gambling has a pernicious effect on one's family, not unlike what occurs with drug addiction. As Mom's gambling profoundly affected Dad, Dianna, and me, so too did Dianna's gambling affect Bob and Krista, and her relationships with them have, at times, been tumultuous.

After my dad retired, he often spent time in Shoreline with my sister. Actually, because she was frequently away gambling, he spent a lot of his time with Bob and with Krista and her family. As had happened with my mom, Dad was taken advantage of by Dianna on numerous occasions, repeatedly bailing her out financially with the hope that she would turn her life around.

Once, when I was in my late forties, Dad knew that Dianna was in severe financial distress from gambling and asked that I travel to Shoreline to check up on her. I didn't have much of a relationship with her at that point, but Dad was really concerned so I did it for him. It was midday when I arrived and Dianna was sleeping. When she woke up, I could tell that she had not showered in weeks. She had a look of desperation on her face, a look I'd seen before. Having been a casualty of my mom's gambling addiction and having borne scars from that experience, I was overwhelmed with sadness. Since Dianna had also suffered from Mom's gambling, I would have thought that she, more than anyone, would have understood the tragic toll addictive behavior has on others. With profound disappointment, I left Dianna some money but decided that I had to sever whatever bit of a relationship I had with her.

For the second time in his life, Dad was personally and profoundly affected by compulsive gambling behavior. As happened with Mom, he was repeatedly let down when he hoped that Dianna's behavior would change if he helped this one last time. Dad finally gave up. When he died, his will included Krista, his two grandkids, and me. Dad didn't trust even a portion of his hard-earned life savings with Dianna.

Growing up, Dianna and I were two peas in a pod. We survived unimaginable hardship. Some might characterize her adult life as one of tragic failure. They would be mistaken. She continued to beat extraordinary odds to educate herself and raise a terrific daughter. Dianna has kept close contact with Dad's family and has a relationship with most of them, whereas I do not, though that is slowly changing. We've taken different paths, but both paths have been filled with positive and negative experiences.

As adults, we had become estranged. The separation began on the day when I learned she was not my full biological sister. We saw each other periodically after that encounter but we never spent much time together. And since that day when I bailed her out of her gambling debt, until recently, we had seen each other only once, when Dad died. We recently spent time together in Youngstown on a fact-finding trip for this memoir and we've communicated more during this past year than we have over the sum of the past fifty years. In reflecting on our past, I've come to better understand the distance she has had to travel to be where she is now. Perhaps, insights gained will allow for a long-overdue reconciliation. I still remember with fondness the six-year-old girl cooking rice for us to eat.

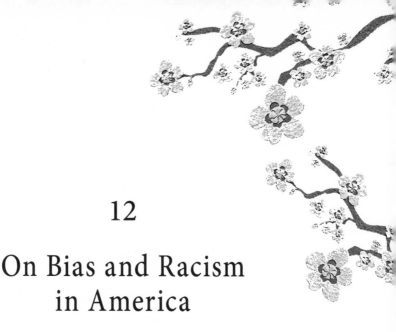

12

On Bias and Racism in America

Growing up, I often wished that Dad was less accepting and accommodating in his dealings with white people. Shortly after we arrived in the United States, my family went on a cross-country trip in my father's Volkswagen Beetle. Some of the communities we drove through had likely never seen a family like ours: a Black man, an Asian woman, and two biracial kids, although Dianna looked more Asian than biracial. One night we stopped at a motel with a brightly lit vacancy sign. After Dad went inside the office to reserve a room, I saw the vacancy sign shut off. Dad came back to the car empty-handed. It seemed obvious that the motel had vacant rooms, and I couldn't understand why he had not been more forceful in securing one for us.

Sometimes my dad seemed resigned to accept his place on the lower rungs of the social class system. I wanted him to be more assertive in claiming his lawful rights and privileges and to demand more respect when it was due. I realize now, though, that he was part of a different generation, one that experienced more outright racism and abuse than did mine. Part of his behavior was probably due to conditioning, but a greater part was likely due to practical considerations of survival.

The history of Blacks in this country is one of chattel slavery from 1619 until 1865, followed by one hundred years of de jure or legal segregation and fifty-five years of equality under the law but de facto segregation in reality. When my dad enlisted, the segregated armed forces had just been integrated by Executive Order 9981. Although I know the history well, I am sometimes still shocked when reminded that states like Virginia still enforced the "one-drop rule" codifying racial classification in law during my lifetime. And when the Supreme Court ruled in 1967—fourteen years after I was born—that laws prohibiting marriage between whites and nonwhites were unconstitutional, sixteen states still had such laws in place. In reality, there was a hierarchy of privilege in his society, and that hierarchy exists even today. The root of that hierarchy is racism.

To be fair to my dad, each successive generation since slavery was abolished, from the mid-1800s through the era of Jim Crow laws to the current time, experienced fewer of the dehumanizing anti-Black assaults upon them than the generation prior. For many people today, the horrific and brutal acts perpetrated against American Blacks—all legally permissible through systems of law and order—are experienced only through books and movies. The images are haunting. But for those who lived through Jim Crow, the experience was terrifying.

Though perhaps not to the same extent as in my dad's generation, I believe that even today, all Blacks experience racism. Some forms are subtle while others are blatant. I can recount my share of both.

In both high school and college, I had teachers who couldn't believe I was getting As and thought there was some sort of grading error or that I was cheating. In high school, a teacher gave me a B in a course I knew I should have aced. When I confronted her about it and we went through each individual grade for every assignment, quiz, and test, it turned out that I had the highest numerical average in the entire class. She changed my grade to an A but could not provide a reasonable explanation as to why she had given me a B in the first place.

I experienced similar incidents in college. During my last two years, I took a lot of advanced courses in mythology, English literature, and philosophy. Once, in an advanced classics course, the professor accused an unnamed student who had received an A of plagiarizing a written assignment. He told us he had even taken a long drive to the larger library in Pittsburgh to try to find the source of the plagiarism, an effort that proved fruitless. He was fishing for an admittance of guilt. I don't know if anyone else in the class received an A on that particular assignment, but I did. As he was talking, he kept glancing in my direction. I felt that he was accusing me, and it was very uncomfortable.

During that same semester, I was taking a small-enrollment course titled the Psychoanalysis of Chess taught by my favorite philosophy professor, Dr. Jim Sheridan. In addition to playing chess and writing about our chess moves, we analyzed the works of Reuben Fine, one of the great chess players of the twentieth century, who also was a psychoanalyst. My chess partner was Rachel, who was white. I thought we were evenly matched, but repeatedly I would put my white Queen chess piece in an unprotected position and Rachel would capture it and win the match. For our final assignment, I wrote about the underlying psychology of Black men and white women in the United States and somehow tied it to Rachel repeatedly capturing my white Queen.

One day, Dr. Sheridan and I were having coffee at a local café and discussing my white Queen analysis when the classics professor stopped by. It turns out the two men were close friends. A few days later, the professor mentioned to me that Dr. Sheridan had remarked that I was one of the best students he had ever had in any of his philosophy classes. That was the stamp of credibility that I had lacked during his rant about cheating. I received an A, not even an A minus, on all my subsequent papers and a rare overall grade of A in his course.

Dr. Sheridan was just one of the many great professors with whom I formed a strong bond at Allegheny. Nevertheless, my time there was challenging. Even though most colleges and universities, including Allegheny, practiced affirmative action and actively recruited Black students, in reality, there were very few on campus.

Being the only Black player on the basketball team was especially difficult. In high school, I was close to most of my teammates. I missed that tight community, the security of knowing that my teammates had my back if I ever needed them and that I had theirs. It didn't help that several of my college teammates were members of Phi Gamma Delta, otherwise known as Fiji, a fraternity well known for its racist behavior.

When I was on my way to basketball practice on Halloween during my third year, one of my Black classmates, Glenda, ran up to me crying. She had just come from the student center, where the Fijis were up to one of their pranks: they were leading one of their members by a rope tied around his neck, his face blackened with charcoal.

When I got to practice, I approached two of my teammates who were Fijis. Despite their affiliation, I kind of liked these two, and thought I had a bond with them. The three of us were the only freshmen to make the varsity team, and one of them roomed next to me in the dormitory our first year. I told them what Glenda had just witnessed, expecting if not a promise to confront their fraternity brothers then at least an expression of sympathy and understanding for her. Their response instead was: "Well, it's Halloween, isn't it?"

That was the proverbial straw that broke the camel's back. I had already witnessed a series of racial incidents, many involving the Fijis, that fueled my disaffection with the basketball team and with Allegheny more generally. In fact, I had already decided to apply to medical school a year early and leave Allegheny because of these experiences.

A few weeks after the Halloween incident, we had a basketball game. The coach and I were having a disagreement over something and he benched me for the entire game. It was a very close game, but the other team was beginning to build a lead. I kept looking at the coach expecting him to put me in. Both Fijis from the Halloween incident were in the game, and one of them was playing the position I would normally have been playing. With less than fifteen seconds left and the game out of reach, one of them fouled out. The coach looked down the bench and told me to go in. I refused and walked off the court. I was not going to be a scrub for that Fiji, particularly since I was the better player. I would rather quit than chump myself like that.

Another incident occurred with a Fiji a few days before my graduation from Allegheny. I was on my way to the dining hall when, without any provocation whatsoever, someone walloped me on the side of my face with enough force that I was knocked down. By the time I got up, the perpetrator had disappeared, but several witnesses were able to identify him. He was a football player and a Fiji. He was also the son of the head football coach, Coach Timer.

That evening, I went to Coach Timer's house to confront his son. I had asked several of my student colleagues from the Association of Black Collegians to wait outside in case I needed support. It was the evening before commencement and the Fiji was graduating. The family was joyous and having a celebratory dinner. At first Coach Timer didn't believe that his son could have hit me without provocation or warning until his son admitted that he had, in fact, done so. I appreciated the Fiji's honesty and willingness to be accountable for his actions, but it was befuddling that he had no rational explanation for them except that he had been drunk and knew I didn't like the Fijis. Coach Timer was embarrassed and offered to compensate me in some way. I had just wanted an apology, which I received, so I walked out of the house. Besides, I thought to myself as I rejoined my waiting colleagues, this would be the last time I ever had to deal with a Fiji since I was graduating also.

Throughout my college career, it bothered me immensely that the basketball coach did not recognize that his only Black player felt out of place with the Fijis. During Christmas break, when the campus was closed, the basketball team played in tournaments and therefore stayed on campus. We stayed at the Fiji house. Although the house was filled mainly with the basketball team, some other Fiji members who had not gone home for the holidays were there. During that entire time, I was constantly subjected to racist jokes and complaints about some of my Black student colleagues. For the entire two weeks, I did not sleep well out of fear that something bad might happen to me.

It is difficult for me to believe that the coach was not aware of the Fijis' reputation. In 1998, Phi Gamma Delta was disbanded by the administration for "multiple violations" spanning many years. It was fourteen years before they were allowed to reestablish themselves, allegedly as a reformed organization.

Almost thirty years after I walked off the basketball court, when I was dean of the medical school at Creighton University, Norm Sundstrom, my old coach, called my office. I still don't completely understand the purpose of his call. He said it was just to "catch up," as if we were old buddies. Norm was now retired and living in North Carolina. He reminisced about the basketball team, and although he didn't outrightly apologize, I sensed regret in his voice. He mentioned something about me being the first Black ballplayer he had actively recruited.

Several years later, when I was living in Denver, I was elected into Sigma Pi Phi fraternity, also known as the Boulé. Founded in 1904, the Boulé is a postgraduate fraternity for which membership is selectively extended to small numbers of accomplished Black men who have a record of demonstrable commitment to the enhancement of Black communities. Through its Mu Boulé Foundation, a nonprofit supported by voluntary contributions from its individual members, funding is provided for student scholarships for promising young Black men as well as for social justice programs and policy initiatives. I had eschewed fraternities in college and vowed never to be a part of one. I made an exception for the Boulé because of its social justice activities. Also, there was no hazing.

Soon after becoming a member, I met Craig Jones, cofounding partner of the wealth management firm Jones Barclay Boston, at a Boulé function. Craig advises active and retired professional athletes. As we were getting to know each other, he seemed stunned by my mention of Suitland and Allegheny. He had played basketball at Oxon Hill, a competitor high school of Suitland, and also at Allegheny, where he knew of me. By the time he played, probably a decade later, he was one of four or five Black players and his experience on the team was very different from mine. I recognized from our conversation how isolating being the "only one" can be and the importance of "critical mass"— not only for basketball teams but in the recruitment of minority students and faculty also.

I did not expect college leadership to take any action, so I didn't even bother to report the Halloween incident and the assault. The sense of helplessness I felt is something that I will never forget. Because of these experiences and the feeling of not being supported by college administration, I decided to leave Allegheny and apply to medical school a year early.

I applied to three medical schools and interviewed at all three: Harvard, Yale, and the University of Maryland. I didn't get into Yale and withdrew my application to the University of Maryland after a bad experience there. Harvard's response to my application was a surprise. I didn't get in, but I wasn't rejected either. Their letter to me was very nice. They commended me on my record but were hesitant to accept a student before completion of an undergraduate degree. I don't remember if I was formally put on the waiting list for guaranteed admittance the following year or not. Nor do I remember the exact wording, but I interpreted their letter as a provisional acceptance pending completion of my undergraduate degree, and this belief allowed me to tolerate the remainder of my college experience.

With regard to the University of Maryland School of Medicine, I was interviewed by a surgeon whose office was filled with photos of horses and hunting dogs. We had a very engaging discussion about horses and a range of other nonmedical topics, and he seemed to like me. And then, with a wide, friendly smile, he compared my behavior and knowledge favorably to that of other Black students. To further amplify his point, he commended my breeding and compared it to that of his hunting dogs.

It was evident from his many photos that he greatly valued his dogs, and I think he meant well. In fact, he probably didn't even know that his comment was insulting and racist. Regardless, I could not see myself in that type of environment and withdrew my application.

I remained at Allegheny to complete my undergraduate degree but my experiences there left scars. I've learned from these experiences, however, and they have helped me develop a greater sensitivity to the needs of minority students and to how university leaders can be more responsive. No student should have to experience what I did, with no one to turn to for assistance.

With time, my feelings about my alma mater have gradually shifted. After all, I received a great education that was the launchpad for a very successful and fulfilling career. In 2003, I was awarded the Gold Citation, "in recognition and appreciation of honor reflected upon the College by virtue of his/her professional activities." In 2016, I visited Allegheny for the first time since my graduation forty years earlier to accept an honorary degree.

～✍️～

In 1986, I moved to Los Angeles to join the faculty at both the Jules Stein Eye Institute of UCLA in Westwood and the King/Drew Medical Center in south-central Los Angeles. I lived in the mid-Wilshire district and to get home from Westwood, if there was traffic, I often drove through the neighborhood of Beverly Hills. As do many people in Los Angeles, I drove a nice car, a black BMW M3; but unlike most people, I got stopped for no apparent reason by the Beverly Hills police on multiple occasions.

Usually, I was nonconfrontational, provided whatever documents were requested, and was allowed to go on my way. On one occasion, things did not go as smoothly. It was 1994 and I had just been promoted to full professor at UCLA, the first (and still only) Black doctor promoted to that level in the Department of Ophthalmology. There was a small office celebration in my honor that I was not expecting at the end of a very long day. The surprise party was a thoughtful gesture of my colleagues and staff, but I was tired and anxious to get home. Driving through Beverly Hills, I was once again stopped by the police, who blared instructions over a loudspeaker and blinded me with their floodlights.

Although I complied with the two officers' instructions, the noise, lights, and commotion were bewildering. They apparently did not consider my explanation that I was just passing through to get to my home in mid-Wilshire and that I worked at UCLA as an ophthalmic surgeon as credible. They demanded that I provide proof of my residence, even though my address was clearly displayed on my driver's license. Although I was in no way aggressive, it's possible that I could have responded with a bit of an attitude. I know now not to get out of the car unless instructed, but I made a mistake and got out. Without warning, one of the officers hit me with his club, threw me up against the car, and handcuffed me.

Things were going downhill quickly. After my initial flash of anger, I felt scared as they aggressively patted me down and searched my car. I felt even more afraid when another patrol car drove up with sirens blaring and stopped in front of us.

Then my fear turned to relief. I knew one of the officers in the car that joined and he knew me. His mother was a well-known resident of Beverly Hills. She had very advanced glaucoma and had come under my care after experiencing complications from glaucoma surgery performed by another ophthalmologist. Her sight was not good enough to drive, so her son often accompanied her to my office. She was very attached to me, and her son was very appreciative of the special care and consideration I gave his mother. "He's good. I know him," he interceded.

I'm not sure what would have happened had my patient's son not arrived at the scene when he did. I admit that I could have been more deferential. However, they never should have stopped me in the first place. I was pulled over because I was a Black man driving a nice car in a nice neighborhood. Further, even if I had violated a traffic rule—which I had not—the aggressiveness of stopping me with sirens and floodlights was totally unwarranted. It was racist.

I often remark that all adult Black men have had some interaction with police that could have turned out badly. The incident in Beverly Hills was not an isolated event; I've had more than a few such interactions. Given my history of being quick to anger, I feel fortunate to have survived relatively unscathed.

I often reacted to acts of racism with anger and defiance. On one occasion, my reaction was one of embarrassment and shame. I had been referred a patient by one of my colleagues, a pediatric ophthalmologist, at the Jules Stein Eye Institute. The patient was an adult with suspected glaucoma, and my colleague requested that I take over his care.

A Shakespearean scholar, the patient was a distinguished-looking man with an imposing, sonorous voice. His speech was flamboyant in style and his choice of words was precise. The initial visit was uneventful. After a thorough evaluation, I confirmed that he had glaucoma and went over a recommended course of action. He seemed amenable and we scheduled a follow-up visit in a couple of weeks.

A few days later, the patient called to cancel his appointment. While that's not unusual, this patient specifically asked to speak to me. I was not prepared for what came next. Basically, the patient questioned my intellect because he thought that my English was flawed. Whether it was an accent he detected or improper syntax or a combination of both, I don't know. What I do know is that he criticized how I spoke, and he thought that my poor speech was indicative of poor intellect.

As a physician interacting with a patient, my options for responding were limited. The patient had every right to cancel his appointment with me and see someone else. Yet, the purported reason for the cancellation, and the fact that he had called to tell me so, was despicable. I wish I could have expressed this to him, but in the moment I felt paralyzed.

Many minorities working in medicine experience "impostor syndrome," a psychological pattern in which individuals doubt their skills, talents, or accomplishments, and fear being exposed as a "fraud." At the beginning of medical school, although I performed well academically, I sometimes had doubts as to whether I really belonged. I overcame that feeling of inadequacy and excelled at every subsequent state of medical training—internship, residency, and fellowship.

At the time of the incident, I was enjoying a very successful glaucoma practice at a leading academic center and was being selected to the list of Los Angeles's best docs and America's best docs annually. Yet, I felt embarrassed by my patient's criticism and perhaps even a bit ashamed. Instead of being able to brush it off, I internalized these feelings and never mentioned the episode to anyone, not even to the referring physician.

I realize now that despite all my successes, this experience scarred me deeply. My response was to work even harder and make sure that there was no doubt that I belonged. As in the past, on so many occasions, I responded by striving to excel.

Decades later, this incident influenced my decision regarding a former Wayne State University student. Martina was a Black employee at Henry Ford Hospital. Because she was talented, CEO Nancy Schlichting had promoted her to the highest level of responsibility she could attain without having a college degree. In advising her to pursue a college degree, Nancy discovered that Martina had earned more than enough credits at Wayne State University to receive a degree years ago but had not received one because she had failed an English proficiency exam, an exam that had been since discontinued. Further, at least part of the reason the exam was discontinued was that many people believed that it was racially biased. When Nancy explained the situation to me, I immediately decided to correct this injustice. Many years after she was denied her degree because of a racially biased English proficiency requirement, Martina marched across the stage at the very next commencement and received her baccalaureate degree.

I'm sure that I acted quickly and decisively because of my own experience with being judged as deficient in English. Black students like Martina—and even accomplished academic physicians like me—have to contend with these types of biases all too often. I'm so pleased that I was able to break down at least one barrier for one deserving person.

Our lived experiences include seemingly innocuous microaggressions in our everyday life: invisibility, success as equated with whiteness, the expectation of race representation. The list goes on and on. The cumulative effect shapes who we are.

In her book *Caste*, Isabel Wilkerson, a former *New York Times* national correspondent and the first Black woman to win the Pulitzer Prize, tells the story of doing a lighthearted article about Chicago's Magnificent Mile and interviewing New York retailers who had decided to move there. In the course of her research, despite having an appointment, one of the store managers refused to see her because he was expecting someone else. Wilkerson wrote: "His caste notions of who should be doing what in society had so blinded him that he dismissed the idea that the reporter he was anxiously awaiting, excited to talk to, was standing right in front of him. It seemed not to occur to him that a *New York Times* national correspondent could come in a container such as mine, despite every indication that I was she."

I understand. Every time a white person looks past me even though I'm the person they desire to see—and it happens far too often—I am dumbfounded.

A decade or so ago, when I was chancellor of the University of Colorado at Denver and Health Sciences Center (later renamed the University of Colorado Denver), I received a phone call from a high-level administrator at an institution in Oklahoma about an urban-serving universities initiative I was organizing. Since I was planning to be in Oklahoma in a few weeks, I offered to meet with him so that we could discuss the initiative in greater detail. We arranged to meet at a local restaurant. I got there a bit early and waited at the bar. The person I was meeting was delayed and was about fifteen minutes late. He rushed into the bar area obviously flustered about being tardy. I was the only person at the bar and I got up to greet him. With hardly a glance, he rushed past me to take a look into the dining room. When he came back out, he again looked past me and asked the bartender if anyone had been waiting for him.

It never occurred to him that the physician and university chancellor he was rushing to meet could be Black. I found the entire interaction off-putting. He was the one who wanted to meet me, not the other way around. I knew how to identify him because I had done a quick Internet search. Why wouldn't he have taken a minute to do the same?

More recently, while president at Wayne State University, a high-level executive who had opened a major business in Midtown Detroit wanted to meet with me. We were both planning to be at an annual conference on Mackinac Island and so we arranged to meet at the coffee shop of the Grand Hotel. When he arrived after me, I approached him and said hello. He ignored me and looked around as if he were searching for someone. I spoke again. This time, at least he didn't ignore me; he informed me that he was waiting for someone and was busy. After the third attempt to get his attention, he finally seemed to realize that I was the person he had arranged to meet.

As with the person from Oklahoma, it is difficult for me to understand how this man, who wanted to meet me, did not know how to identify me. I knew this was the man I was supposed to meet when he was still twenty yards away. More disturbing is that it took three attempts to get him to realize that the person he was brushing off was the person he had arranged to meet—at his request.

~~~

Systemic racism is deeply embedded in academic medicine and academics more generally. I love academics and have devoted my entire career to it. But this injustice must change. The hierarchical nature of relationships places those on the lower rungs of the academic ladder in a position of vulnerability to abuse and harassment from those on higher rungs. Underrepresented minorities—Black, Latino, American Indian, Native Hawaiian, or other Pacific Islander—disproportionately make up the lower rungs and are disproportionately impacted. Consequently, underrepresented minorities make up less than 10 percent of medical school faculty and 15 percent of university faculty, whereas they represent 32 percent of the U.S. population. A much smaller proportion of underrepresented faculty make up the upper ranks of professors, department chairs, and other administrative leaders.

Even those who have navigated the systemic barriers to succeed in this system are prone to individual acts of harassment from higher-ranked administrative leaders who harbor racial biases or racist views. After having reached the highest levels of academia, I still had to deal with such harassment.

One of these incidents occurred when I was the chancellor of the University of Colorado Denver, the top official presiding over both the general academic campus in Denver and the health sciences campus in Aurora. Bruce Benson was the president of the three-university system, which included the University of Colorado at Boulder and the University of Colorado at Colorado Springs, in addition to the University of Colorado Denver.

During one of our routine update meetings, he surprised me with the result of a secret audit he had conducted of my university business expenses.

Curiously, I was the only one of the three chancellors (the other two were white) of the University of Colorado system that he audited. I do not know with certainty if Benson was a racist or not, but at the very least, his action was influenced by racial bias. The impetus for this audit was that a Black city government official had recently been accused of misusing public funds for private purposes, a story that made news headlines for days. Benson's biases may have led him to rationalize that he was protecting the university by making sure that the Black chancellor was not doing the same thing.

Benson had personally reviewed all of my expenditures from the beginning of my position as chancellor to the time of that meeting, a span of over three years. As the leader of a major university with a budget of over $1.5 billion, I typically had dinner or reception events four or five times per week, including weekends. And out of the hundreds of dinners I hosted at my home during this time, only three were with Black guests. The two events he questioned were among these. The issue was not the cost of the dinners, which was minimal, but the pocketbooks of my Black guests. "Why are you spending university funds on these two guys?" he challenged. "They don't have any money." I was dumbfounded. While it may have been true that neither was rich, both were highly respected and influential thought leaders in Denver: one was the editor of Denver's main newspaper, the *Denver Post*, and the other was the Denver city planner. As chancellor, I cultivated a lot of friendships and raised a lot of funds for the university, and I also entertained many white guests who did not have a lot of money.

I was so stunned that I didn't think to ask him for a copy of the spreadsheet he had in front of him that listed all of my expenses. I expressed my surprise that he would bring up these two minimal expenses out of hundreds. Perhaps realizing by now that these were both prominent Blacks with deep community connections and that the expenses were entirely appropriate, Benson got a bit flustered and quickly put away the documents.

The next day I received a visit from Benson's chief of staff, who tried to clean things up. He knew that Benson erred in singling out these two expenses and was probably concerned that I might publicize it. This time I did ask for a copy of the spreadsheet, and, though it was promised, I never received it.

The chief of staff explained that Benson wasn't questioning the justification for the university expenditures but believed that university general funds rather than development funds should have been used. For a number of reasons, including how business expenses were processed by the university, this explanation made no sense. Benson's biases had been exposed, and this was just one of many indignities I endured with him. From that time forward, I insisted on being audited quarterly, rather than annually, a practice that I continue to this day.

I didn't fit Benson's image of a leader and I knew he felt more comfortable with people who looked like him and shared his worldview. Knowing also that he was capable of unethical acts, such as attempting to take public credit for donations for which he was not involved, I resolved to leave the university. Several years later, after I had left and after my position was split into two positions filled by two of his good ol' boys, he reportedly commented that now he had Coloradans in each of his major leadership positions. Colorado does not have a lot of Blacks. Many people, including me, took his comment regarding Coloradans as code for white.

Systemic and individual racism poses many barriers for the advancement of Blacks and other minorities in academics. It happens at all levels, from students to university presidents and chancellors. Having endured such injustice, I am committed to fighting against it so that other minorities can have an equal opportunity as whites to succeed.

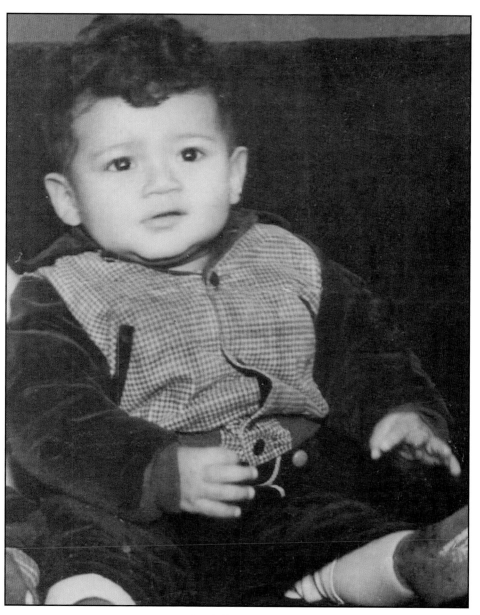

As a baby in Japan.

Dianna, 1967.

Mom, approximately 1964.

Dad, as young man, 1949.

"Hey, I dare you to say we ain't the best."

Suitland's basketball team after a victory.

Ms. Stephan and me in
eleventh grade, 1971.

Marina and me at high
school senior prom, 1972.

Sophomore student at
Allegheny, 1973.

Graduation from Allegheny College, May 1976—
Dad, Mom, and Aunt Mabel (Dad's aunt).

Dad, Mom, Dianna, and Dianna's daughter, Krista, 1982.

With Presley, 2003.

With Yoshio, 2004.

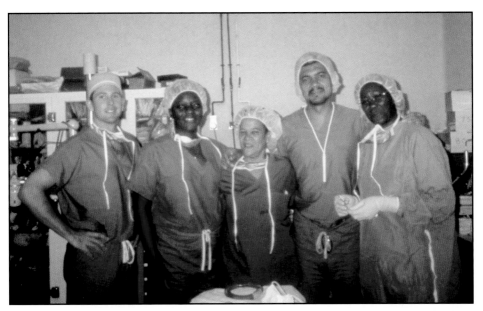
Operating room of Queen Victoria Hospital in Castries, St. Lucia, with nurses and trainee. Dr. Sade Kosoko is second from left.

Field training of Cameroonian team members, 1991.

Survey methodology training of Cameroonian team members
with WHO consultant Serge Resnikoff, 1991.

Receiving honorary degree, Allegheny College, 2016.

Consummating partnership between University of Colorado Denver and Dar Al-Hekma University with Zuhair Fayez. Jeddah, Kingdom of Saudi Arabia, 2005.

After AAMC Chair Address at 2018 Annual Meeting—Jacqueline, Yoshio, Presley.

Inauguration as twelfth president of Wayne State University.

Wayne State fundraising event with Jacqueline. With us are Chief of Staff Michael Wright and his wife, Connie, 2014.

Core group, Road Warrior Cycling Tour, 2019. From left to right: Joe Vadnais, me, Rob McGregor, and Don Rose.

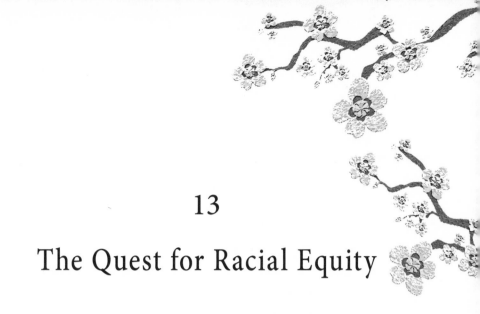

13

The Quest for Racial Equity

Anti-Black racism is a real scourge that must be addressed. But it is important to consider how we go about seeking justice. Many years ago, as a freshman at Allegheny, I went to a protest that had been organized by a group of upper-class Black schoolmates. I didn't know much about the protest at the time, but we marched to the college president's house, and the leader of the group demanded that the president come out and speak to us. When he did, the leader of the group and several other upperclassmen yelled at the president, called him demeaning, disrespectful names, and made a series of demands. Apparently, the group wanted a Black modern dance troupe from Cleveland to perform at Black History Week, and not enough funds had been allocated to bring the dance troupe to campus. I don't recall the president's response, but I actually don't think he was given much of an opportunity to even speak. After witnessing this spectacle for a few minutes, I left, unable to condone it.

I later decided to become a leader in the Association of Black Collegians (ABC) and became president of ABC during my junior and senior years. Allegheny didn't have a lot of Blacks during my time there. In fact, from 1972 through 1976, the year I graduated, there were a total of only fifty-five Black students. But our influence grew. For Black History Week during my senior year, with the support of the president of the college, the ABC hosted the premier Black modern dance company in the country, the Alvin Ailey American Dance Theater.

I realized, after that protest as a freshman student, that change was not going to occur through name calling and threats against those with the power and influence. There can be no denying that white people have historically been responsible for perpetrating unspeakable atrocities against Blacks; but not every white person is responsible for these actions and not every white person is racist. Yet, some Blacks will not work with whites to attempt to find solutions and will even attack other Blacks who do.

Recently, two very prominent white colleagues separately confided in me that they did not understand the Black Lives Matter movement and wanted me to explain it to them. Both were people I respected and did not believe to be racist. They were sincerely trying to understand. But it was difficult for them to reconcile the desire to attain equity and justice and to effectuate positive change with the actions of some Blacks who looted, damaged property, and caused personal harm. I tried to explain the underlying cause of the movement: the deep distrust of many Blacks of institutions, policies, and practices that have devalued their worth and their lives; that police interactions with Black people, including teenagers, too often resulted in fatal shootings while white people, even when attacking the police, typically go home to their families unharmed; how the disproportionate killing of Black people makes them feel that their lives do not matter. The Black Lives Matter movement posits that Black lives matter just as much as the lives of everyone else—that it was not a binary choice between Black Lives Matter and All Lives Matter. Of course, all lives matter; but Black lives matter also, and that fact seems to have gotten lost in the more inclusive slogan of All Lives Matter. Both of these colleagues listened, and maybe they understood.

Detroit has a large majority Black population of around 80 percent. As would be expected with such a large population, Blacks occupy many of the leadership positions in the city and region. Also, as would be expected, these leaders are nonhomogeneous with respect to many attributes, philosophies, and approaches to problem solving. Some are uncompromising and combative;

others are collaborative and inclusive. Although I prefer dealing with the latter group, I do understand—even if I do not agree with—those who espouse a more confrontational approach in their quest to achieve a more radical agenda. I believe, though, that both groups truly desire to make meaningful change for the betterment of their communities. I may not agree with their tactics, but I don't doubt their motive.

During my time at Wayne State, currently nine years at the time of this writing, the more confrontational group had no shortage of complaints and voiced them at meetings of our university's governing board, at protest marches, and at press conferences. Although Wayne State is the most diverse university in Michigan and among the most diverse research universities in the country, some felt that our student population should racially mirror the population of Detroit.

Facts often didn't matter—for example, when a group of Black community activists complained during a 2018 press conference about the lack of Black students in our medical school. This was puzzling. The number of underrepresented minorities in the class that had matriculated in the fall 2014 was low, with only seven total, five of whom were Black. Immediate action had been taken, including changing the leadership ranks of the school, and the class entering in the fall 2016 had increased to sixty-one underrepresented minorities, thirty-one of whom were Black. The numbers of underrepresented minorities and Blacks in the subsequent years were similar. The class entering in fall 2018, the last class admitted at the time of the press conference, had thirty-three Black students, an almost sevenfold increase from 2014. Aside from the few medical schools categorized as an HBCU (historically black colleges and universities), these data placed Wayne State among the top five medical schools in the country in terms of Black student enrollment. I have no problem with those who espouse that we must strive to do even better no matter the improvement. But to not even acknowledge progress—to be charitable—undermines their credibility.

Detroit also has Black leaders who are among the most inspirational and effective change agents I've met anywhere. Many, though not all, are affiliated with the

Black church. Detroit has more than twenty-five hundred Black churches, and the leaders of these churches have tremendous influence within their communities.

One such leader, Reverend Wendell Anthony, is the pastor of Fellowship Chapel and president of the Detroit chapter of the NAACP. I met him early in my presidency of Wayne State. Reverend Anthony was an alumnus and he cared deeply about Detroiters. He was no-nonsense and very clear about his expectations of Wayne State to serve the community and broader Detroit. Reverend Anthony felt that we needed more Blacks at Wayne State and that we needed to serve Black students better, but he was also pragmatic and understood that it would take time. Most importantly, he was willing to be a partner in achieving these shared goals. My experience was that Black leaders like him far outnumbered and were far more influential in promoting progress for Detroiters than the confrontational ones.

I would also place in this category of effective and influential leaders who positively impact their communities the members of the Detroit chapter of Sigma Pi Phi fraternity, or, as mentioned previously, the Boulé. Members of this esteemed fraternity include trailblazing Black leaders from a broad spectrum of politics, health care, and business. When I moved to Detroit, I transferred my membership from the Denver chapter to the Detroit chapter, and it has been my privilege to be a part of this fraternity with some of the most committed and accomplished Black men of Detroit.

The murder of George Floyd, and others, by the police has awakened the American consciousness to issues of systemic racism and structural inequities. It has stirred among many Americans, white and Black, the desire for social justice and racial equity. Much work has yet to be done to redress the atrocities of slavery and of Jim Crow. It can't be done without the active support and participation of the entire range of society, including white people. To make true progress in leveling the playing field for all Americans, it is imperative that we get the right people on the bus and ignore the wrong people.

Young people, including college students throughout the country, have led the way in protesting racial inequities and demanding social justice. These people, of all races and ethnicities, will not accept the status quo, nor should they.

We need their passion and sense of indignation at the current state of affairs regarding racial diversity, inclusion, and equity.

Black college students particularly, including college athletes, have been especially active in demanding change, and many universities, as well as the larger society, are responding. Although there is a cultural divide in our country and overt racism seems to be on the rise, I am heartened by the broad support for Black Lives Matter and other racial equity issues.

My hope is that these enthusiastic young people keep their eye on the ball and don't get distracted by their own personal agendas. I once encountered a situation wherein a former president of the Black Student Union (BSU), who enjoyed being the center of attention, actively worked to undermine a newly elected president of the BSU. The new president resigned from her leadership role in the BSU and started a new student group with a mission and goals that overlapped substantially with those of the BSU. I do worry about such counterproductive behavior—in this case by both the former and new presidents of the BSU. Blacks and other minorities may be at an inflection point in achieving some successes, but real progress will require the support of a broad segment of society, from grassroots to grasstops. The credibility of all of us who are involved in the quest for racial equity, which has thus far been elusive, must be unassailable.

I've grown wary of the ability of many large organizations to drive change toward racial equity, as again and again I've seen how they purport to want change but fail to implement it. In 2017, I attended the annual conference of the NCAA in Nashville, Tennessee, during which the main plenary session was about diversity. In addition to a white male, the panel consisted of a white female and a white male gay person. Here's an organization that has been accused of exploiting college athletes, many of whom are Black, and criticized for having inadequate racial diversity in the leadership and coaching ranks, and yet there was not a single Black person on the panel. I sat near a group of Black student athletes who were looking at each other throughout the session as if asking, "*What about me?*" Maybe some in the audience believed that having a gay person and a woman on the panel represented diversity, but the entire session struck me as tone deaf.

Another experience I had with the NCAA was even more disappointing. The dearth of Black males in medicine has long been, for me, a societal issue of concern. In 2018, only 2.8 percent of medical students were Black men; in 1978, when I was in medical school, 3.4 percent were Black men. In stark distinction, the matriculation of Black women into medical school has improved considerably over this same forty-year time period.

In 2019, I saw an opportunity. Along with Hannah Valantine, the Chief Officer for Scientific Workforce Diversity at the National Institutes of Health (NIH), I conceived of a partnership between three major national organizations, with the goal of increasing the numbers of Black males going into medicine: the Association of American Medical Colleges (AAMC), where I was chair of the board of directors; the NIH, where I was a member of the Advisory Council to the Director, the highest-level advisory council at the NIH; and the NCAA, where I was a member of the Council of Presidents for Division II, the highest governing body for collegiate Division II athletics. As a result of my leadership positions, I was aware that both the AAMC and the NCAA, Division II, had substantial reserve funds, and I believed that this money should be spent on a substantive initiative that addressed a societal need. The leadership of the NIH, the AAMC, and the NCAA enthusiastically endorsed the partnership and the plan.

Both the NIH and the AAMC were eager to get started. The NCAA initially voiced support but ultimately became a barrier to implementation. The thwarting of the project happened in stages. First a lawyer from the NCAA expressed concern about potential Title IX and affirmative action lawsuits, a consideration that was not believed to have much merit according to most legal experts. Then, even though the Council of Presidents had voted to use a portion of their reserves to initiate the project, this decision was successfully appealed by the Management Council of the NCAA, a governance group made up of athletic directors, faculty advisory group members, and representatives from the senior women administrators. A representative from the Management Council, who was a woman, disagreed with the focus on Black males and argued that women and other minority groups should be included. Further, she argued that focus should be on the broader group of student-athletes who were struggling to complete college rather than the more select group of student-athletes who may aspire to go to medical school.

These arguments were rational. Regarding the focus, I would argue that this is a uniquely Black male problem and that it is becoming a national crisis. Precise focus was necessary to address it. More expansive programs to improve the graduation rate of Black and other minority student-athletes are also important. However, most colleges and universities have robust programs for improving the baccalaureate graduation rate of Blacks and other minorities. More to the point, no one had proposed a specific project to address this problem at the NCAA level. Getting more Black males into medical schools versus getting more Blacks to graduate from college was a false choice. In reality, the choice was getting more Black males into medical school versus doing nothing consequential. I was concerned that these reserve funds would not be used for anything strategic but would just be frittered away by providing each Division II college or university a proportional rebate as had been done the prior year.

The Council of Presidents deliberated on the appeal by the Management Council and the funding recommendation was reversed. As I feared, the bulk of the reserve funds were allocated to the individual Division II institutions, a mere $3,459 to each. For most universities this amount would barely register a blip in the overall budget and would certainly not be sufficient to undertake a substantive diversity and equity initiative. What a squandered opportunity! Despite all the talk of the greater importance of assisting Black student-athletes to graduate from college, there still is no such NCAA-funded program to do so.

Following this decision, several NCAA leaders—most notably Brian Hainline, the NCAA's chief medical officer and the person whom Mark Emmert, the CEO, had assigned to the project—wanted to move forward with some discretionary funding that could be made available for a more modest initiative until another attempt at more robust funding could be made the following year. Unfortunately, the Covid-19 pandemic ensued. Both the NCAA and the AAMC incurred substantial financial losses as a result of the pandemic, and even the more limited funding became unavailable. The initiative I organized was made possible by the unique circumstance of my having leadership positions at all three organizations and by the fact that the organizations had significant reserve funds at that time. Such an opportunity would likely not come up again for quite a while, if ever.

I believe that the leaders of the NCAA are well-meaning and concerned about racial equity. As individuals, I think they desire to do something to address it. However, as a large, bureaucratic national organization, systems of bias are well entrenched operationally. If this period in our history is to lead to substantial progress in achieving some level of racial equity, my bet is on the passionate advocacy of students and other young people rather than on bureaucratic institutions like the NCAA.

~~~

Progress on racial equity everywhere has been slower than many of us would like, but there has been progress nonetheless. I witnessed one example of this in 1995 when I traveled to South Africa with a small group of Black university leaders and politicians to explore partnership opportunities with several South African institutions. It was post-apartheid, and though living and working conditions for many Blacks were still deplorable, the conditions were slowly improving. One particular event provided hope to those of us privileged to witness it. We were invited to a "reconciliation" graduation at the medical school of the University of Natal, later named the Nelson Mandela School of Medicine, in the city of Durbin. All Black and other nonwhite graduates of the medical school who had not been able to participate in commencement during the apartheid era were invited to march across the stage and have their diplomas handed to them by the vice-chancellor, Brenda Gourley.

I watched as Black and nonwhite graduates of the medical school proudly marched in academic regalia across the stage to receive their diplomas. The commencement address by Gourley was extraordinary; she apologized and unequivocally stated that how the medical school had treated these graduates was unacceptable.

Closer to home, I am reminded of the surgeon at the University of Maryland who compared me to his well-bred hunting dogs. Sixteen years later, in 1991, the University of Maryland School of Medicine appointed Donald Wilson as dean, the first nonminority medical school to appoint an African American to that top leadership position. Don and I overlapped as deans of nonminority medical schools—I was the dean of the medical school at Creighton from 1998 to 2003—and we often joked that I was his little brother because we shared the same last name.

Don retired as dean in 2006 after a successful fifteen-year tenure at the helm of the medical school. The university initiated a search for Don's replacement, and I was aware that Albert Reece was a candidate. Al had a distinguished career as a physician and was dean of the College of Medicine and vice-chancellor for medical sciences at the University of Arkansas at the time. He is also Black. As deserving as Al was of being appointed as Don's replacement, I really did not believe that the medical school would appoint another Black man to this leadership position. I was wrong. Al was appointed dean of the medical school and vice president for medical affairs at the University of Maryland School of Medicine in 2006. The school from which I withdrew my application because of concern about the racial climate has had thirty-one consecutive years of leadership under a Black man as of this writing. Progress has been slow, but racial equity is undeniably improving.

My dad died before Barack Obama was elected president of the United States. He did not believe a Black man would ever hold the position. During the early part of Obama's campaign, Dad did not consider him as a serious candidate. Later, when it became obvious that he was, he feared for Obama's life. He just couldn't fathom white people allowing a Black person to become president.

Many people interpreted Barack Obama's election as a sign of a "post-racial" United States, a society in which racial prejudice and discrimination no longer exist. Conservative talk-show hosts and news anchors latched on to this term eagerly. Most Blacks didn't buy it. That race still matters was unintentionally spotlighted by Chris Matthews, an MSNBC host, when he gushed of President Obama, "He is post-racial by all appearances. You know, I forgot he was Black tonight for an hour." The implicit message: there's something wrong with being Black.

Let's not be lulled into believing that racism is over because a Black man was elected president of the United States. We still have a long way to go to achieve a post-racial society. In 2003, when I was interviewed at a press conference announcing my appointment as the incoming president of Texas Tech University Health Sciences Center, the first question I was asked by a local reporter was, "How does it feel to be the first Black person to lead this university?" I'm usually not at a loss for words during interviews. In this case, I really didn't know how to respond.

As long as race makes a difference in our society, we should acknowledge, and even embrace, this reality. Tremendous progress in advancing racial equity and in reducing bias and discrimination has been achieved from the time of Dad's generation to mine. I expect continued progress through subsequent generations. Ultimately, I believe we will have a post-racial society, but not until the stark realities of racism and racial inequity are acknowledged and addressed.

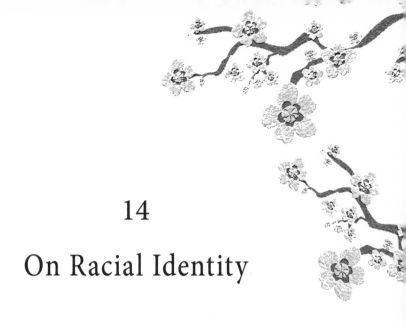

14

On Racial Identity

The construct of race forms the foundation upon which racism exists. Race is a complex concept, and the color of one's skin inadequately defines it. Evelyn Brooks Higginbotham, a noted Harvard historian, once quipped, "When we talk about the concept of race, most people believe that they know it when they see it but arrive at nothing short of confusion when pressed to define it."

As someone who is biracial, I've thought about race a lot and have written and lectured extensively on the topic of race in medicine.* In the United States, race is predominantly a social and political construct born out of our nation's history. Since race has no basis in biology or genetics, with definitions that change periodically and differ geographically, the gold standard for racial classification is self-identity.

As a young man, I did not know many Black Asians. The few I did meet did not identify as Black and none were my friends. The exception was Shinzato Porter. I met Shinzato through a mutual friend who had attended the University of Pennsylvania with him. After Penn, Shinzato received an MBA from UCLA and began working at one of the big investment banks on Wall Street.

---

* M. Roy Wilson, "What Is Race?" *International Ophthalmology Clinics* 43, no. 4 (2003): 1–8; M. Roy Wilson, "The Use of 'Race' for Classification in Medicine: Is It Valid?" *Journal of Glaucoma* 12, no. 4 (2003): 293–94.

The friend thought that Shinzato and I had a lot in common and introduced us as I moved from Boston to New York City to begin my medical internship.

Having grown up in a Black neighborhood in Philadelphia, Shinzato was the first Black Japanese I met who identified as Black and was also comfortable with his Japanese heritage, as evidenced by his insistence on being called by his Japanese name. His older brothers, George and Rick, ran the streets of North Philly, and both died young. They wanted a different life for Shinzato and had made sure he went to college.

After leaving Japan to go to high school at Suitland, I had abandoned my Japanese heritage. Shinzato's self-confidence and comfort with his identity helped me to reconnect with my Asian culture. His influence is at least partly responsible for why I eventually added "Masao" to my legal name.

I appreciate, and even cherish, my Asian heritage, but there's no confusion about it: I identify as Black. I identify as Black partly because society has told me I am Black and society has treated me as a Black person. There was a time when I was upset with people like Tiger Woods, who tried to downplay his Black identity, even coming up with a new word, Cablinasian, signifying his Caucasian, Black, and Asian heritage. I always thought that the "one-drop" rule would have classified him as Black in a previous generation. And even though the "one-drop" rule is no longer legal, I knew that society would revert to this principle and treat him as Black if he were to ever lose some of his star power. Sure enough, when he got into trouble with his white wife, Elin Nordegren, and his infidelities with other white women were exposed in 2009, the media portrayed him as just another Black thug.

Despite our nation's long tradition of drawing sharp lines between racial and ethnic groups, our ancestry is fluid and complex and how we self-identify is influenced by our lived experience. I'm biracial and identify as Black. Tiger Woods is biracial and identifies as Cablinasian.

I no longer give any thought to biracial people like Tiger Woods who do not fully identify with being Black. After all, he is from another generation, one that has not routinely experienced the same indignities experienced by Black people of my dad's generation, and even by mine to a lesser extent. My own children, Yoshio and Presley, who have three Black grandparents, do not see race through the same lens as Blacks in my generation.

The greater transgression, in my opinion, is purposefully misrepresenting one's race or ethnicity for personal gain. During the Jim Crow era, light-skinned Blacks sometimes tried to pass as white. Given the deplorable treatment of, and lack of opportunities for, Blacks during this period, this misrepresentation is understandable. More difficult for me to reconcile is a white person falsely claiming to have Native American or Latin heritage. Such claims can sometimes be difficult to disprove, and there are real consequences to such fraud since it may cost real Native Americans and Latin persons access to higher education and other opportunities. Having been involved with admissions at many levels of education, including undergraduate schools, medical schools, and postgraduate residencies and fellowships for many years, I have noted such misrepresentation becoming more commonplace, and I deplore it.

The situation with Rachel Dolezal, who made headlines in 2015 as a white person trying to pass as Black, is unusual. The controversy over her racial identity led to her resignation as president of the NAACP chapter in Spokane, Washington. While I don't condone what she did, the ensuing media attack was unjustifiably harsh and often based on a complete misunderstanding of the meaning of race. One particularly misinformed column was published by the *Detroit Free Press*. I was so bothered by its mischaracterization of race that I wrote a rebuttal op-ed. Unfortunately, the *Detroit Free Press* chose not to publish it.

In their haste to criticize Dolezal—and I have no issue with that—the media propagated false information. For example, the *Free Press* column asserted that Dolezal's parents were "bewildered by her gene denial" (as if there was a gene for being white), bemoaned the fact that "what you feel trumps what science says you are" (as if science dictates a person's race), and insisted that Dolezal was "rejecting biological details" (as if race is a biologic variable). Here are the facts: race is not genetic, it is not scientific, and it is not biologic.

The article went on to quote a Fox News commentator who likened the scenario to a person identifying as a cat. It was difficult to discern whether this cat analogy was meant seriously or offered in jest. If the columnist thought of it as legitimate, it was ignorant; if he was purposefully making a ludicrous comparison to emphasize some point, it lacked journalistic integrity. Felines comprise a different species than humans. All of humankind, whether Black, Caucasian, or Asian, are members of a single species, *Homo sapiens*, distantly distinct from the thirty-seven species of felines. If he actually thought Dolezal identifying as Black is comparable to a woman identifying as a feline, he likely watched one too many *Catwoman* movies.

I condemn intentional racial or ethnic fraud. A white person passing as Native American or as Black has the privilege of doing so part-time. Growing up, Native Americans and Blacks suffer discrimination and racism that most white people never have to face. With the possible exception of European Jews, they don't have to suffer the sequelae of ancestors struggling for survival against genocide or experiencing the degradation of slavery. They can enjoy the benefits and sidestep the generational handicap of their newly assumed identity.

But I also condemn misinformation about the meaning of race. Race is primarily a social construct. While it has no genetic or scientific basis, the concept of race is important and consequential. Societies use race to establish and justify systems of power, privilege, and oppression. In truth, it should be acknowledged that claims of race being "biologically meaningless" are not totally accurate. Yet, the fact that self-identification has not been superseded as the basis for categorization reflects the fluidity of race and the overriding influence of the psyche. Society assigns us a race at birth, and it becomes part of the subjective consciousness of the individual. For the most part, we are what we say and believe we are.

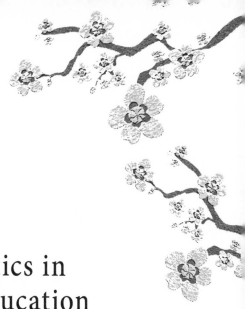

15

On Politics in Higher Education

I am often asked what the most difficult part of being a university president or chancellor is. These are challenging jobs. In fact, the job of a university president or chancellor is arguably more difficult than that of the CEO of a large corporation.

University presidents/chancellors, who are functionally CEOs of their institutions, have much less power and authority than CEOs from just about any other industry. Consulting with faculty is not only expected but required before many decisions of any magnitude are made. Increasingly, other university constituents, including students, alumni, and community members, desire a seat at the table and expect to be consulted. Being held solely responsible for outcomes, while having to share authority for decision-making with others, is disconcerting. A colleague of mine once quipped that his job was dependent on the unpredictable behavior of a bunch of eighteen-year-olds. Although perhaps said in jest, the sentiment does have an element of truth to it. Unquestionably, though, the most difficult aspect of being a university president is dealing with partisan politics.

I recall a conversation over a decade ago with my friend Michael Drake, when he was dealing with a particularly difficult situation as chancellor of the University of California, Irvine. The university had been embroiled in controversy related to Muslim students protesting against perceived injustices perpetuated by the Jewish community. Michael had declined to censure the student group as demanded by Jewish faculty and students, thereby upholding the value of freedom of speech. This response angered the Jewish community, including Jewish members of the university's governing board. I remember thinking that getting in the middle of such a long-standing conflict as that between Muslims and Jews was a no-win proposition, and I was thankful that I had not had to deal with that issue during my university presidencies.

That would soon change. On May 10, 2021, an outbreak of violence commenced in the ongoing Israeli-Palestinian conflict. Over the next eleven days, both Hamas and Palestinian Islamic Jihad launched a bombardment of rockets, and Israel began a campaign of airstrikes against the self-governing Palestinian territory of Gaza. By the time of a May 21 ceasefire, 256 Palestinians, including 66 children, were killed; in Israel, 13 people were killed, including 2 children. With such tragedy, it is difficult to maintain objectivity. For many people, Israel was clearly at fault for the conflict; for others, Hamas instigated it.

Wayne State's Student Senate issued a statement condemning Israel and showing support for the Palestinians, who suffered disproportionately in the conflict. This action by the Student Senate elicited a predictable response from the Jewish community, within Wayne State and in the region, which demanded that I denounce the Student Senate action. The university did not allow the Student Senate to use the university-controlled student listserv, so their statement was publicized only through social media. Nonetheless, some took the statement as representing an official Wayne State position.

Members of our governing board called me, and some wanted to issue a statement from the board. However, as individuals, their views on the Student Senate action and on the conflict were not uniform. One thing that could be agreed upon, though, was that the Student Senate did not speak for the entire university.

After extensive discussions with my senior cabinet, I decided to issue a statement that communicated the following: (1) support for freedom of speech and the right of the Student Senate to express their beliefs; (2) clarification that the Student Senate statement was not a university statement; and (3) an expression of regret that the students had used unnecessarily inflammatory language (ethnic cleansing) in their statement.

Within hours, I received dozens of emails and phone calls in response to my statement. About half of them believed that I had not gone far enough and that I should have denounced the Student Senate; the other half believed that I had gone too far in criticizing their action. I knew that issuing a statement of any sort was going to be a no-win proposition. I could have stayed silent on the issue and it may have blown over eventually. That's not leadership, though, and I did what I thought was the right thing without regard to potential political ramifications.

Some level of politics is unavoidable in higher education; it has always been embedded in American colleges and universities. Critical thinking and free speech, foundational elements for colleges and universities, also inform the national discourse on a wide range of topics, including some that cross into politics. Where, until recently, politics did not blatantly influence university operations and policies, it is now infused into all aspects of higher education, particularly in public colleges and universities. Support of something as basic as the value of a college degree has become a partisan issue. Partisan politics influences who gets selected to lead universities, which institutions are rewarded with state funding support, what topics are allowed and disallowed in the curriculum, and which faculty get or are denied tenure.

In 2006, I was selected as chancellor of the University of Colorado Denver and Health Sciences Center by Hank Brown, the university system president who previously served in the U.S. Senate as a Republican, and a majority Republican board. I never felt—not even an inkling—that politics had entered into my selection as chancellor. My interviews focused on my past experiences and accomplishments and on how I might put those to work in serving the university.

Since that time, the selection process for the University of Colorado's leaders has become increasingly political. Bruce Benson, whom I mentioned previously, was selected as president by a majority Republican board after Hank

Brown retired. Benson had been president of Colorado's Republican Party, but he did not have a terminal degree and otherwise lacked the usual credentials to be president of a highly reputable university system. Bypassing a formal search process, he hand-selected loyal friends who shared his conservative worldview to lead the Denver and the health sciences campuses.

In July 2018, Benson announced his intent to retire, and the politicized process for the selection of the university system leader was repeated. During the search for Benson's replacement, I received a surprise phone call from a well-known Republican politician. The search firm had requested that he be a candidate for the system presidency. Knowing of my history at the University of Colorado, this person thought that I might be able to provide some insight into the position. Most of all, he was perplexed as to why he had been contacted since he lacked educational leadership experience of any sort, and he wanted my opinion. Given his strong Republican credentials, I thought the answer was obvious. Fortunately, he possessed enough self-awareness of his strengths and weaknesses to decline the invitation. I think that he dodged a bullet.

The board eventually selected Mark Kennedy as president by a partisan 5–4 board vote with a Republican majority in May 2019. Kennedy was a former right-wing politician who served in the U.S. House of Representatives from 2001 to 2007. His higher education résumé was relatively weak, and there was a huge outcry from faculty and students when he was hired. He never gained their trust and confidence, and he had a short and tumultuous tenure as president.

In January 2021, the board switched partisan control for the first time in forty years, with Democrats in the majority. Five months later, Kennedy announced he was stepping down. In his announcement, he alluded to political pressures, stating the "board has a new makeup this year that's led to changes in focus and philosophy."

The University of Colorado is one of the few universities in the country whose board of regents, the governing body, is elected by the public. But university boards with appointed members can also become entangled in politics. The board of the University of South Carolina is made up of the governor (or governor-designated appointee), the state education superintendent, sixteen members appointed by state lawmakers from each of the state's judicial circuits, and the president of the Alumni Association.

Robert Caslen was selected as president of the University of South Carolina in July 2019, despite not possessing an earned doctorate (a published requirement of the position), and overwhelming opposition from faculty and students ensued. He was appointed on a split 11–8 board vote after intervention of the chair of the board and governor of the state. The tainted search prompted a formal investigation from the university's accrediting body, the Southern Association of Colleges and Schools. After a series of gaffes, Caslen resigned from the presidency after less than two years in the position.

As unseemly as these examples of political influences may be, at least the selection of university presidents is in the purview of governing boards. Political interference in curricula and tenure decisions—which should be in the exclusive domain of faculty and provost—degrades the academic enterprise and undermines the credibility of university leaders. Take, for example, the recent case of Nikole Hannah-Jones's tenure. The tenure approval process is typically routine and warrants little public attention: a recommendation is made by the faculty to the provost, and the board of trustees accepts the recommendations of the faculty and provost. For Nikole Hannah-Jones, a Black Pulitzer Prize–winning journalist and lead author of the *New York Times Magazine*'s politically charged 1619 Project, it was anything but routine. In May 2021, the University of North Carolina at Chapel Hill's board, whose members are appointed by the Republican-controlled legislature, chose not to act on the tenure recommendation to avoid angering a wealthy, conservative white donor who was critical of the fundamental tenet of the 1619 Project, which situates the nation's history in the context of slavery. After a national outcry, the board reversed its decision and awarded her tenure, which she declined. In his public statements, the chancellor, Kevin Guskiewicz, walked a fine line. While saying that he wanted Hannah-Jones to join the faculty, he did not criticize the board for its initial inaction on her tenure. In her statement, Hannah-Jones took aim at him: "When leadership had the opportunity to stand up," she wrote, "it did not." At the same time, the board was upset with the chancellor's support of Hannah-Jones, however muted.

Another politically charged situation is that of Boise State University in Idaho, where Marlene Tromp took over as president in July 2019. It's been a balancing act for her ever since. As conservative Republican legislators have tried to wrest millions of dollars of state support, explicitly as punishment for the institution's social-justice programming, student activists have become more strident about injustices they see on campus. In trying to avoid angering both groups, Tromp was placed in an increasingly untenable situation as ideologically based demands have left little room for compromise. Unthinkable a decade ago, college leaders elsewhere are now facing similar predicaments.

The Covid-19 pandemic has exacerbated such partisan tensions. That institutional policy has been influenced by politics is evidenced by examining the correlation between the political power base of states (red state or blue state) and institutional mask and vaccine mandates, with public higher education institutions in blue states more likely to issue such mandates and those in red states resisting, even in the face of mounting evidence of the need for them.

At North Idaho College, the president, Rick MacLennan, decided to impose an indoor mask mandate because of a predicted surge in Covid cases. Shortly after he announced the mandate, the board voted 3–2 to rescind it. Due to tensions between the president and the three board members on this and other related matters, they voted to terminate him, without cause. The same majority then selected the college's wrestling coach, who had no college leadership experience (beyond his time as wrestling coach) as interim president.

In Michigan, in response to a late summer surge of cases due to the Delta variant, the three research universities—University of Michigan, Michigan State, and Wayne State—issued a vaccine mandate in preparation for the fall semester and on-campus instruction. This action was immediately met with a threat from the Republican chair of the House Appropriations Committee that state funds might be withheld in retaliation for the mandate. Interestingly, all three universities are led by presidents who are physicians, and we acted, consistent with our medical training, in the interest of health and safety. As the pandemic worsened, other public universities in the state also issued vaccine mandates. Ultimately, the state legislature did not financially punish universities that imposed vaccine mandates, but it did insert legislative language into the final budget bill that made it easier for individuals to be exempted from vaccinations.

Like it or not, politics has become an increasingly bigger part of the job of a university president. As the country has grown more politically polarized, so too have higher education institutions. Throughout my academic leadership career, I have tried to stay clear of politics. Most people do not even know my political party affiliation. That's because I'm difficult to pin down as simply a Democrat or Republican. I hold both Democratic and Republican views on many issues.

Many people assume that I am a Democrat because of my liberal social views. But I'm also financially conservative and hold several more traditional Republican views on other issues. Despite my personal negative experiences with police, for example, I am not a proponent of "defunding the police." Like what America used to be, I'm kind of down the middle and eschew viewpoints from both the extreme right and the extreme left. Regardless, I've always believed that my personal political views should be kept separate from actions and decisions made on behalf of the university I am charged to lead. I believe this separation to be important, but it has become an increasingly utopian view.

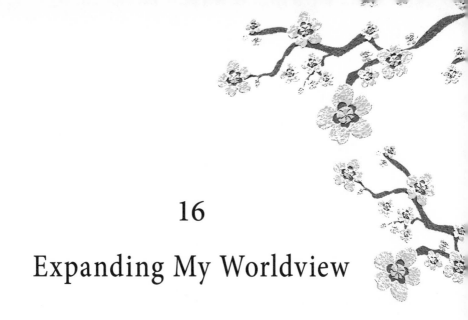

16

Expanding My Worldview

I did not—and still do not—take for granted the opportunity I was provided to go to college and to medical school. Although I felt that four years of college was akin to being in purgatory, I absolutely loved my time in medical school. To be able to look out into the future and know with certainty that I was going to have a career where I could so positively impact people and also earn a good living was exhilarating.

My experience at Harvard Medical School (HMS) was positive from the start. The interview for consideration of admission was conducted by David Hubel, a famous brain scientist who would later win the Nobel Prize in Physiology or Medicine in 1981 for discoveries concerning information processing in the visual system. Sitting across from him in his office, located on the imposing HMS Quadrangle, was unnerving, but he put me at ease. Because of my interest in the brain from a psychoanalytic perspective, I probably knew more about his work than the average college student who was trying to get into medical school, and we had a terrific conversation.

I arrived at Harvard in the fall of 1976. Many of my classes were taught in the Ether Dome, the operating amphitheater where surgical anesthesia with inhaled ether was first publicly demonstrated in 1846. It was awe-inspiring. For someone who went to a public high school known mainly for its athletics, it was also a bit intimidating.

Allegheny had prepared me well, however. All first-year students had to take a biochemistry placement test during orientation week. The night before the test, I reviewed a biochemistry book, although I understood that cramming for such a test was likely futile. Surprisingly, some of the topics I happened to review were on the test and I therefore knew the answers. I'm not sure if reviewing the subject the night before the test was the reason, but I was one of only a few students who tested out of first-year biochemistry and was placed in an advanced class instead. Yet, despite the fact that I was clearly capable and deserving of being at HMS, I wondered—as happens with many minority students—if a mistake had been made. It was my first taste of imposter syndrome, an affliction that I would suffer from for only a few years.

The fact that I felt inadequate is understandable, given the accomplishments of many of my classmates. Most medical students complete their four years of college at age twenty-two or twenty-three and begin medical school immediately thereafter, whereas most of my classmates were older by about three or four years. Many were accomplished in other disciplines outside of medicine and science and had remarkable pre-medicine experiences. Among my classmates were Olympic athletes, world-class concert musicians, novelists, and poets. Some of my classmates not only had published scientific articles as undergraduates, a significant accomplishment in itself, but had already published a book. One had studied traditional Chinese medicine and wrote a book about it, in Mandarin, and he wasn't even Chinese!

One way I relaxed after major exams was to get in my car, put on a tape of Keith Jarrett's *Köln Concert*, and drive north out of Boston. Staying predominantly on local roads and with no specific destination in mind, I would explore towns such as Salem and Amesbury. One day I came across Phillips Academy Andover and was astonished. I had heard of Phillips Academy but to actually see a high school with such resources was breathtaking. The grounds were expansive, larger even than those of many colleges, including Allegheny, and picturesque. Unlike Suitland, which consisted of a solitary, nondescript building, the many Georgian-style buildings dotting the campus were breathtaking. Many of my medical school colleagues had gone there or to similar high schools such as Phillips Exeter Academy. I wondered how I could ever compete.

On one of my trips after an exam, I noticed a horse-riding academy in the town of Andover. I had loved reading the Black Stallion series as a kid in Japan and always wanted to learn how to ride horseback. I began weekly lessons at the stable and became fairly proficient, even learning how to jump. Over several years, I made frequent trips to Andover for my horseback-riding lessons. If time permitted, I would make a slight detour and visit the Phillips Academy campus and wonder what it would have been like to go to high school in a place like that.

Forty-four years after I first walked the grounds of Phillips Academy Andover, Raynard Kington was announced as its sixteenth Head of School, the first person of color to hold that position. I had collaborated with Raynard on several community-based research projects when I was the dean of the School of Medicine at Charles Drew University of Medicine and Science and he was a faculty member at UCLA. Raynard left UCLA because—inexplicably—he did not receive tenure in the medical school even though he was well funded through several NIH grants and was very highly regarded. He later went on to have a distinguished career in research and higher education (deputy director of NIH and president of Grinnell College) before joining Phillips Academy Andover.

Raynard and I have maintained contact over the years. As college and university presidents, we were very familiar with elite university preparatory boarding schools, although both of us went to public high schools. When I received the announcement, I was so proud that a Black man, who like me was a physician and higher education president, was now leading this historic institution. I recalled how I had once walked its campus, wondering if I could compete with students who attended such a school; I never imagined that a friend and colleague would one day become its leader.

My first friends at HMS were three Black guys in my class—Neil Powe, Herman Taylor, and Ernie Carter. Each had excelled academically growing up and had graduated from prestigious universities. Neil and Herman had received their undergraduate degrees from Princeton, and Ernie had obtained an under-graduate degree from Harvard and a doctorate degree in bioengineering from the University of Pennsylvania. I was a bit intimidated by their intellect at first but soon realized that they were just regular folks who happened to be really smart and worked hard through school. We became study partners and a friendship grew out of that shared experience.

We all lived in Vanderbilt Hall, the dorm for the medical students, our first year. Herman and I rented an off-campus apartment together our second year. During gross anatomy, the four of us worked on the same cadaver. I gravitated to the head, Herman to the upper chest area, and Neil to the lower abdominal area. Ernie was kind of all over the place. Interestingly, I became an ophthalmologist (eyes), Herman a cardiologist (heart), Neil a nephrologist (kidneys), and Ernie became Health Officer of the Prince George's County Health Department.

Election into the National Academy of Medicine (NAM) is one of the highest honors in the field of medicine. Neil and I were elected in 2003 and Herman in 2020. There are probably sixty Black members who have been elected to NAM over the past several decades. Three of them worked on the same cadaver as first-year medical students.

One of the things I value most about my time at HMS were the friendships I developed with other males. To this day, I don't have any friends from childhood, high school, or college. In childhood, I didn't develop any lasting friendships because I moved often; the glue that bonded us in high school was athletics and we all went our separate ways after graduating; and in college, I studied all the time and didn't socialize much.

One of my friends from high school was Kenrick Stephens. Kenrick and I played football together, but we also took several classes together. He was the only football player who was at the same level of math as I was, and we often compared notes. Kenrick became a pharmacist and worked at the pharmacy at the Walter Reed Hospital in Washington, D.C., when he recognized my dad's name on a prescription order. Kenrick got my contact information from Dad and we connected.

Kenrick had settled in the Upper Marlboro area of Maryland, near Washington. On one of my frequent visits to D.C., I went to visit him. I enjoyed catching up with him. After high school, he went to an HBCU in Florida, where he starred as a defensive back. I was pleasantly surprised as he described how he had developed tremendous speed—4.4-second 40-yard dash—after high school and made his college football team as a walk-on. I was surprised because in high school Kenrick was slue-footed and had a slow, lumbering gait with his feet pointed outward.

Because my relationship with Kenrick had been based on both athletics and academics, I had more in common with him than with anyone else in high school. Yet, I realized during this visit that we now had very little in common. As we sat in his living room sipping beer from a can, his young daughters peering around the corner to get a glimpse of their father's high school friend, I became acutely aware of his shotguns and rifle hanging along a wall. He was a hunter. Not only had I never hunted, I had never even fired a gun. That was just one of the many differences between us I began to notice, some of them superficial, such as the type of beer we preferred, and some more substantive, such as our view of and interest in global issues. Once Kenrick had updated me on the status of mutual friends and colleagues we had in high school, there was not much else for us to talk about.

I genuinely enjoyed seeing Kenrick. But I also realized that the only thing we had in common now was a shared past. This visit revealed the stark reality that I had no friends from high school.

College was no different in that regard. There were only a few Black students on campus. Although I was friendly with them, I didn't become close friends with any of them. I had an academic agenda and my focus was on accomplishing it, leaving little time to nurture relationships. The closest thing to a friend I had was Charlie Craik, a white guy from a working-class background, who was probably more driven to accomplish academically than anyone I knew, including me. Charlie was so distraught over not being valedictorian that he refused to participate in commencement. He would often comment that his goal was to receive the Nobel Prize in Chemistry. He hasn't achieved that goal yet, but he has had an extremely successful career as a chemistry professor at the University of California, San Francisco, and elected member of the American Academy of

Arts and Sciences. I understood his compulsion to excel and occasionally we would go out to eat or just talk.

Medical school was different. As a second-year student at HMS, I met Barry Jordan, a first-year student who would become one of my closest lifelong friends. Barry was from New York. Although both of his parents were alive, he had been raised by his grandmother because his parents had been unable to. Despite his difficult life circumstances, he excelled academically at Stuyvesant High School, a preparatory magnet public school that consistently ranks among the best in the country, and attended the University of Pennsylvania.

The thing that attracted people, including me, to Barry is that he was cool. He took care of business but also enjoyed life. The antithesis of the stereotypical medical student, he did what he had to do academically to advance, and even to excel, but he also knew how to have fun. The trait I loved the most about him though was that he could rap to struggling working-class people from the neighborhood one minute and converse with highfalutin folks with money and power the next without missing a beat. Despite his successes, Barry was one of those people who never forgot the circumstances from where he came and embraced it.

Through Barry, I met several of his classmates, including Rick Baker and Jose Calderon, who were his friends. The three of them became my "boys," a term of endearment we reserved for the closest of friends. Jose was proudly Puerto Rican, but he had a darker skin tone and we just considered him Black. Like Barry, Rick and Jose were from New York (Rick from Harlem and Jose from Coney Island) and had overcome difficult life circumstances to excel academically and make it to HMS. The details differed, but each of them—as did I—persevered through daunting life challenges that would have derailed most young people. Yet, we were all at HMS, and that unlikely probability was the foundation of our bond.

Becoming friends with these schoolmates gave me a new perspective on the exacting circumstances of my childhood. I would undoubtedly have preferred a less fraught one, but I realized that we had learned some valuable and highly transferable survival skills. Few of our colleagues at HMS had experienced the same degree of trauma and suffering as we had. They likely didn't have absent parents; they hadn't dealt with unsafe neighborhoods; they hadn't been subjected to racial profiling and harrowing police encounters; they hadn't battled negative perceptions and biases just to get to the starting line; they didn't have to continuously prove that they belonged.

And yet, whatever our history, we were now all at the same place. I—and my boys—may have had to travel further than our colleagues and may have had more barriers to overcome, but we were now all students at HMS. That had to count for something. And if whatever strength of determination, street smarts, and survival skill that got us to this point could be marshalled yet again when necessary, would we not have an advantage over our colleagues in prevailing over future adversities? I believed that we would. That belief bolstered my confidence, and I've never looked back.

Let me be clear. I am not saying that we were all equally academically prepared or were equally smart at HMS. I marveled at the intellect of some of my colleagues, and still do. As a second-year student, I was once forty-five minutes late to a test I had assumed started at 9:00 a.m. Entering a hall full of test-takers at 8:45, I realized my mistake; it had started at 8:00. The test was scheduled to conclude at noon so it was reassuring to see that one of my classmates, Jake Joffe, had already completed the test and was leaving. About five minutes later another student, Steve Hyman, also turned in his test and walked out. Three hours later, I was still in my seat struggling to complete the test before the time limit. It was a long test. To this day, I still don't understand how anyone could have completed the exam so quickly. Even if all I had to do was read the questions and not answer them, I doubt I could have finished the exam in the allotted time.

It takes more than being really smart and a fast thinker to achieve career success. As would have been predicted, both Jake and Steve have had very successful, even extraordinary, careers. But that is not always the case. I have witnessed medical students, ophthalmology residents, and glaucoma fellows who were super smart but became paralyzed when confronted with a setback. An ophthalmology resident I knew, who trained at a very prestigious, selective residency program, gave up when she failed to get into a specific glaucoma fellowship program. Always a brilliant student, she had never experienced failure and just couldn't handle it. She never regrouped to apply to another program and abandoned her goal of becoming a glaucoma specialist.

Getting to know people like Barry, who overcame extraordinary life circumstances, affirmed for me that my own experiences, even the negative ones, gave me an advantage for the future, everything else being equal. I approached the remainder of my medical school and subsequent medical training secure in my abilities and confident that I would prevail in overcoming any and all obstacles.

As important as this insight was to my subsequent career, I owe Barry something more—the ability to open up and to trust. During medical school, I dated a number of women. By this time Marina had moved to Boston and was in and out of the picture, although I was trying to move on. One of the girls I dated occasionally from Harvard Business School got pregnant and wanted to get an abortion. I was distraught with the entire situation and confided in Barry.

Marina somehow found out and was livid. We had both been seeing other people, so she had no right to act as she did. She probably still held out hopes of us getting back together, though, and she was very angry. I remember her banging on my apartment door, yelling at me and causing all kind of ruckus. Although there was no need for me to feel cowed, her rage was intense and I couldn't face her.

I was also feeling rage, but it was directed at whoever divulged this personal information to Marina. I wanted to find this person; I'm not sure what I would have done, but it would not have been nice. After much thought, I realized that the only person I had told was Barry.

With this realization, I immediately calmed down. I remember thinking to myself that Barry would never do anything to purposely hurt me. Though I didn't understand why Barry would have told Marina something so private, I trusted that he had his reasons. I had to take a leap of faith. I dealt with Marina as best I could and supported the other woman through her difficult ordeal as she underwent an abortion.

Several years later, during my internship in New York City, Barry and I went to get breakfast after a night of partying. Although we had been up all night, we talked for hours about our Boston experiences. During our conversation I discovered that he wasn't the one who had told Marina about my private matter. To this day, I don't know how she found out. I'm glad that I thought it was Barry, though, because through that ordeal, I came to understand the value I placed on true friendship.

❧

There was another lesson about success that I learned at HMS: the importance of "playing the game." After one of my first clinical rotations, I spoke to the faculty preceptor about my grade; I had been given a "satisfactory" ranking but I believed that I had merited an "honor." I had taken good care of my patients, had developed a trusting relationship with them, was always on time, and did everything that was asked of me. As I made my case to him, he looked at me as if I was clueless. Without spelling it out, he told me that I wasn't even close to receiving an "honor" grade.

There was really no way I could argue with the faculty preceptor since there was no objective way of assessing my performance. The difference between a "satisfactory" and "honor" was largely based on perception. I thought back to the performance of one of my colleagues on the same clinical rotation who had received an "honor" and tried to compare myself to him. He didn't work any harder than I did or put in more hours, but he always seemed to be in the right place when the faculty preceptor was around. He also seemed to know the right things to talk about. It was obvious that the faculty preceptor liked him. When we were on call, I would typically spend my time looking after my patients—checking on them, speaking to them, answering questions. I never saw my colleague on the patient floor; he was always in the library.

That's when I realized that there was a game being played and that there were certain behaviors that had to be adopted in order to get "honors": during rounds, cite as many articles, especially from the *New England Journal of Medicine*, as you can that are relevant to your patient's condition; if you really wish to impress, cite articles relevant to your colleagues' patients also; don't show up for rounds on time—come a few minutes before the faculty attending. Most importantly, if a faculty attending asks you what specialty you will be pursuing after medical school, the correct answer is always whatever rotation you are taking at the time. If you are taking pediatrics, you want to be a pediatrician; if you are taking a surgery rotation, your dream has always been to be a surgeon. For a bonus, know about your faculty attending's publications and find a way to cite them. For double bonus, throw in that you are interested in pursuing research in the faculty person's area of interest.

My problem wasn't that I didn't know how to play the game; I didn't even know that a game was being played. Once I understood how it worked, I received my share of "honors."

The game didn't end once I completed medical school; it just changed. I now always advise students, "If you don't know that there is a game being played, you will lose out." Whatever the circumstance—medical school, academic promotions, appointment to national committees and boards—if you wish to succeed, you must understand that there is a game being played. Learn the game, and then play it well.

Although most of my memories of medical school are positive, I lost two classmates, one during medical school and one after we had graduated. Carol committed suicide during medical school. I knew her fairly well. She had strong opinions and a dominant personality that was hard to ignore. Attractive and smart, she seemed to have everything going for her. The entire class mourned her loss. Another good friend and classmate was a woman named Pam. As a Black student, she was part of a small group of us who studied and socialized together. During our second or third year, Pam was diagnosed with multiple sclerosis, an autoimmune disease that attacks tissues in the brain and spinal cord. Pam had always dreamed of becoming a surgeon and decided to pursue general surgery, a physically demanding specialty even for someone completely healthy. The rigors of surgery proved to be insurmountable and she switched her specialty to rehabilitation medicine before dying shortly thereafter from complications of MS.

It is so easy to forget those who are no longer with us. Like many others, I am guilty of discarding memories of unfortunate occurrences, such as a death, that make us uncomfortable. Both of these women were too young to have died; both had extraordinary potential that was never realized. What a loss for society.

In every institution I've had the privilege of leading, there was a student death, either by suicide or through unexpected illness. Each time this happened, I reached back in time to relive my own experiences with the loss of a colleague. Each time, I felt for the students who had lost a colleague. Some deaths are unavoidable, such as with Pam. Others might have been avoidable, as with Carol. We must pay more attention to those that may be avoidable and support our students' mental health needs. As a university president, there is nothing more tragic than the loss of a student life.

✍

Among the many clinical rotations in medical school, the surgery rotation was the most rigorous. For two months, it was every other night and every other weekend on call. We had one free half day every other Sunday.

HMS had a strong bias toward academic careers and toward internal medicine and general surgery. There was an unspoken expectation that students would pursue postgraduate training in internal medicine or general surgery and then go into academic careers to become chairs of departments and deans of medical schools. One of my study partners was going to pursue internal medicine. I felt pressure, both from her and from the medical school, to pursue general surgery. To make matters even more difficult, I had received honors in my advanced surgery rotation, and there was a realistic chance that I would match for my residency at one of the Harvard-affiliated hospitals, which were among the most prestigious surgery residencies in the country.

But I felt ambivalent. Part of my uncertainty stemmed from my experience of having only half a day off every other week during my surgery rotation. I couldn't imagine doing that for five or six years, though I've never shied away from long hours and hard work. During my entire career, the times I've taken a real vacation, rather than just a few days tacked on to the beginning or end of a medical meeting, have been few.

My decision was ultimately based on a desire to be true to myself, to not be influenced by outside opinion or lured by prestige. I realized that part of the reason that I considered surgery stemmed from a tendency to compete, to pursue a specialty that was as prestigious as (or more prestigious than) what my study partner was pursuing. What she admired about me, though, was that I had always danced to the beat of my own drummer, that I didn't necessarily conform to expected behavior. I dated girls I met at parties who did not go to Harvard or MIT; I lived in neighborhoods like Beacon Hill and Back Bay where no other medical students lived; and I shopped at Louis, the most exclusive men's clothing store in Boston.

I was one of ten in my class to match into ophthalmology. That was a large number for HMS; usually only a few pursued this specialty. The dean for medical education, Dr. Dan Federman, was alarmed when the residency match list came out, revealing the large number of students pursuing ophthalmology. Believing Harvard's reputation rested on the number of students placed in prestigious internal medicine and general surgery programs throughout the country, he called a meeting of HMS faculty to discuss how such a thing could have occurred and to ensure that it didn't happen again. On the other hand, he was pleased that my study partner had matched in internal medicine at a very prestigious teaching hospital and even called to congratulate her. This gesture reminded me of how teachers in grade schools reinforce the behavior of their favorite students. Like a teacher's pet, she grinned with pleasure and a sense of accomplishment when she received his call. Then, halfway through her first year of postgraduate training, she realized that she didn't like internal medicine and switched to another specialty, one that would not have met Federman's approval but has given her an extraordinarily successful and fulfilling career.

By the time I completed medical school, I knew I wanted to specialize in ophthalmology and subspecialize in glaucoma care and research. After medical school, further training is typically obtained through an internship and residency. Ophthalmology has an early match system, so I knew I would be performing my ophthalmology residency at Harvard's Mass Eye and Ear Infirmary (MEEI) before I had to rank my choices for where to perform my medical internship year. Having spent four years in Boston for medical school and anticipating another three or four years at the Mass Eye and Ear Infirmary, I decided to go somewhere with a predominantly underserved population in a large urban setting. I was pleased to match for my internship at the Harlem Hospital Center in New York City.

New York was certainly a different experience both socially and professionally. In the summer of 1980, I moved into the Lenox Terrace apartments on the corner of 5th Avenue and West 135th Street, about a block from the hospital. The Lenox basketball court was situated between the hospital and apartment, and the Harlem YMCA was about two blocks away. I was in basketball heaven.

Harlem Hospital had a basketball team that participated in a citywide hospital league. I made the team—the only physician on the team—and despite the fact that I was a medical intern with a crazy schedule, I was able to arrange things so that I played in most of the games. The games were at night so it was not a problem when I was not on call. It was a bit more of a challenge when I was on call. A few times, Brenda McCoy was my supervising resident, and she allowed me some flexibility to be absent for a few hours as long as my patients were stable and I was all caught up with my work.

Brenda had an interesting history. Prior to medical school, she had danced with George Faison, a well-known Black dancer, artistic director, and theater producer, and she looked and moved like a dancer. Brenda had a boyfriend named Ty who was not on her level educationally or socioeconomically. I recall him being an ex-offender or reformed gangster, but he seemed to be a good guy and they had a great, mutually supportive relationship. That's what I found so refreshing about Brenda; she was very secure with herself and didn't care about things others cared about in judging people. Brenda just did her own thing, and I respected that about her.

One day when we were sharing stories at work, she described a fishing village in Portugal she had once visited. The scene seemed idyllic. Getting up early in the morning and walking on the beach as the fishermen came in with their morning catch, she would watch as they emptied their nets and sold the fish to local restaurants. I made a wistful comment about living the simple life and how wonderful it all seemed.

Brenda said something that has stuck with me ever since. "It seems wonderful, Roy, because you don't have to live the life of these fishermen, out alone in the sea most of the night. It's a postcard scene for us, but it's a matter of survival for them," she gently chided. "They don't have a choice." Years later, when I visited the fishing villages that dotted the St. Lucia coastline, I would reflect on that comment.

I met a lot of interesting people in New York and had a great time. But I had a double life. During the day and when I was on call, I was a medical intern. At night, I would hang out with a totally different crowd, people I had met through nonmedical acquaintances, and party, often until the early morning hours. One of my favorite places was the Ice Palace on West 57th Street, a gay nightclub with great dance music. I usually went there with my Puerto Rican friend, Nancy, who often remarked that the only group who got treated worse than Blacks and Puerto Ricans were the gays and lesbians, so they just didn't give a f-ck and just wanted to party. The Ice Palace would close about 3:00 or so in the morning and we would move on to an after-hours club called the Garage, a place so dark that I would always be surprised to walk out into the light at the end of the night. I saw a lot of sunrises coming out of the Garage that year.

Looking back, I could easily have gone off the rails during this time. What kept me at least somewhat grounded during that year was my girlfriend, Cyrene. I met Cyrene at a party celebrating my graduation from medical school. The party was held on the top floor of the Royal Sonesta on the Cambridge side of the Charles River, and about a hundred or so people were present. Before it concluded, I noticed two women heading for the elevator to leave. One was the most gorgeous woman I had ever seen. I had never done this before, but I actually ran to the elevator to get her name and phone number.

Cyrene had come to the party with a friend of a friend who knew me. She had just graduated from nearby Northeastern University and was returning to her home in Teaneck, New Jersey, just outside New York City. That was great since I would be performing my internship in New York City in a week or so. On our first date in New York, I took her to see Akira Kurosawa's epic movie *Kagemusha*. A lot of guys wanted to date her, but no one had ever taken her to see a Japanese movie before. She thought I was interesting and we started dating. Cyrene had a quiet confidence about her, and, as her name might connote, her aura was serene. She was a calming influence during a very hectic year.

After my internship year, Cyrene briefly moved to Boston with me but then moved back to New York. I don't remember the exact reasons, since we really cared for each other, but I was focused on my ophthalmology training and she had a difficult time breaking into the job market.

I visited Cyrene off and on during long weekends from work. She was living in the same apartment complex, on Lenox and 5th, where I had lived as an intern, and was modelling. Although Cyrene was older than most models, Eileen Ford of the Ford Modeling Agency had shown interest in her. Because she was competing with girls many years younger, she rarely wanted to go out to dinner because of her dieting and she typically went to sleep early to look her best. Eventually, I stopped visiting and we drifted apart. Cyrene's father died of lung cancer shortly afterward. His funeral was the last time I saw her.

I'm sometimes amazed at the energy I had in that stage of my life, but I'm certainly glad for the experiences, which brought me into the company of two broad groups of people, none of whom were in the fields of medicine or science. One group was comprised of accomplished people in the creative arts: primarily dancers, actors, and musicians, many of whom I met through Brenda and Cyrene. Less constrained by societal norms than my medical colleagues, many led openly alternative lifestyles. They were great at what they did, but what they did was different from what I was doing.

The other group consisted of talented and very special people who did not attain the levels of formal education that many of my other friends and acquaintances had. One of them was Nancy, who did not go to college but is one of the most intuitive and gifted people I know. I'm convinced that she can do anything she sets her mind to. I met her through one of my boys from HMS, Jose, with whom I shared an apartment during my third year of medical school. Nancy often came up from New York to visit him. The kind of bond I had with friends like Jose and Barry was that any friend of theirs became my friend and, vice versa, my friends became their friends.

During my first weekend off in the beginning of my internship, I went to visit Nancy at her apartment in the Bronx. Jose's sister, Juanita, was Nancy's good friend and she was also visiting. I was so tired that I fell asleep on the living room couch while we were all talking. The next thing I knew, it was the following morning. I had slept for nine hours. Somehow, the two women—each of them not weighing much over a hundred pounds—had dragged me to bed, made sure I was comfortable, and had Café Bustelo coffee ready for me when I awoke. Nancy had taken care of me. Since then, we've taken care of each other.

Let me be clear—Nancy and I never had a romantic relationship. She's always been like "one of the boys" to me. The reason I appreciate her so much is that she would always ground me and make sure that I never acted like I was special because of my education or accomplishments. If I did, she would correct me. As with Barry, Nancy allowed me to be comfortable just being me.

In truth, there were times during the subsequent four decades when I did pull away because of my position as dean of a medical school or president of a university and I believed I was supposed to act in a certain way and have certain friends with certain qualifications. Nancy was unlike the people I was associating with on a daily basis; she didn't fit the mold. But each time we reconnected, I would be reminded of how special she was as a person and as a friend.

I am fortunate to have had other Brendas and Nancys in my life. What I've learned is that life is so much more enriching when we are open and welcoming to people who do not share the same background or experiences. One of my colleagues at the NIH always concludes her presentations with the sentiment "Great minds think differently." Embracing differences has indeed helped me to grow, both personally and professionally.

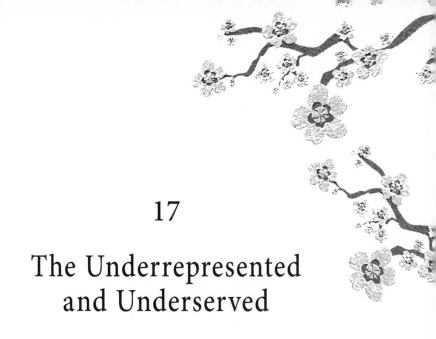

17

The Underrepresented and Underserved

When I decided to go to Harlem for my internship, I had a vague idea that I wanted to work with underrepresented and disadvantaged populations. But at the time, I knew nothing about "health disparities" and didn't even know what that meant. I learned about the preventable differences in the health status of different populations, which became an area of focus in my career, because of my internship at the Harlem Hospital Center.

I went to medical school at a place commonly referred to as the "Mecca" of medical care. The patients were primarily white and economically stable, and the resources were vast. I didn't even have to draw blood on my patients; an expert phlebotomist was available to do so for us. The situation at Harlem Hospital was different; resources were limited and interns often had to perform duties typically handled by other health care personnel. This was before Harlem became gentrified, and the patient population at the hospital was exclusively Black, poor, and very sick. While they received terrific care from the doctors and nurses, much was beyond their control.

My experience working in the emergency room was particularly enlightening. One of the perversities of our health care system is that people without health insurance are often relegated to using the emergency room for their routine care. I consequently managed a lot of patients with problems stemming from chronic disease in the emergency room because they lacked other avenues of medical care. I remember one patient in particular, a young man named Luke. He would come in on a routine basis and I got to know him well. Luke had ascites, a buildup of fluid in the belly due to severe liver disease. He didn't have money or health insurance, so I would often give him a supply of diuretics (water pills) to help flush the extra fluid from the body. In order for diuretics to work, they must be accompanied by a restrictive diet that is low in salt. For Luke, maintaining a low-salt diet was impractical; he ate whatever he could to keep from going hungry. His fluid would consequently come back, and I would have to perform a paracentesis—a procedure in which a large needle is inserted into the belly—to remove the excess fluid.

Near the end of my internship, after I hadn't seen Luke in a while, I learned that he had died. His liver disease had progressed to the point that he had complete organ failure. I couldn't help but wonder if the outcome would have been different for someone with the same condition but more resources, including health insurance. Such a patient would not have been getting episodic care in an emergency room but would have been under the watchful supervision of a primary care doctor as well as a liver specialist. They would have had access to more definitive but expensive treatments, such as a shunt or liver transplant. The reality was that our medical system is not organized to provide such care to poor Black people with no financial resources.

Although I wasn't aware of the term "racial health disparity" at the time, situations such as these ignited my interest in the underlying social determinants of health.

After completing my ophthalmology residency and glaucoma fellowship in Boston, I went to St. Lucia in the Caribbean islands. Both my clinical work and research conducted there reinforced my interest in health disparities and working with underserved populations. But it was my next job, as chief of ophthalmology at the Charles R. Drew University of Medicine and Science (CDU)

and the King/Drew Medical Center (KDMC) in Los Angeles, that solidified my interest.

The KDMC rose out of the ashes of the Watts Riots of 1965. When the root causes of the race riot were investigated by a governor-appointed commission, lack of health care in the region was identified as one of the inciting factors; the closest major public trauma center was located over ten miles away. In 1966, a task force was established to develop a full-service community and teaching hospital operated by the County of Los Angeles in conjunction with the UCLA Medical School and the newly formed Charles R. Drew Postgraduate Medical School (later renamed the Charles R. Drew University of Medicine and Science), a private, nonprofit medical school with a mission to train doctors to work in areas of urban poverty.

I concluded my work in St. Lucia in June 1986 and started my new job in Los Angeles a month later. Many people in academic ophthalmology wondered why I took the position as chief of ophthalmology at KDMC when I had other very attractive opportunities. Some thought it presaged a premature end to my career. After all, the residency program at the KDMC was on probation and under threat of losing its accreditation. The program had attracted negative media coverage and the previous chief of ophthalmology was given a one-year sabbatical with the explicit understanding that she was not to return.

In November 1986, just months after I began my position, the Accreditation Council for Graduate Medical Education (ACGME) was scheduled to visit again. Since the program was on probation, it would be terminated if the residency review was not successful.

Almira Cann, who was the first Black ophthalmology resident at UCLA, had recently completed her residency training there and had been selected to be the interim chief of ophthalmology. She had begun the preliminary work of identifying potential residents and faculty before my arrival and stayed on for several months afterward to assist in my transition before returning to her clinical practice in Pasadena. There were several Black ophthalmologists in Los Angeles at the time and some had received their training at the KDMC. Along with the residents and one or two white ophthalmologists, they leaned in with a common purpose. The ophthalmologists took time away from their own practices to help supervise and teach the residents. Saving the residency program was the primary goal. But it was more than that. It was also about the patients who depended on our services.

The patient population we served was similar to that at Harlem Hospital. They typically had advanced disease, and glaucoma was especially problematic. Because glaucoma is a chronic disease, glaucoma patients went to the clinic often and became well known. Mr. Morrison was one such patient. He had presented to the clinic with very advanced glaucoma in both eyes. After months of treating him with medication, glaucoma surgery was deemed necessary and he was scheduled for a trabeculectomy. Mr. Morrison didn't show up for his surgery.

Several weeks later, I was cycling in the vicinity of the hospital and turned down a residential side street to avoid some heavy traffic. I saw an older man in his yard watering his garden and said hello. It was Mr. Morrison, so I stopped and spoke to him. When I asked about his no-show status for surgery, he replied, "Doc, I can see okay. I don't think I really need surgery." After I explained to him that glaucoma was a silent thief of sight and that he was losing sight without realizing it, he said something that impacted me greatly. "Doc," he said, "if you want me to have surgery, I'll do it." Mr. Morrison was going to have surgery on his eyes, not because he believed he needed it but because I wanted him to and he trusted me. That responsibility weighed heavily on me and has impacted my approach to each patient I've ever had the privilege of treating.

Mr. Morrison had glaucoma surgery performed in both his eyes. Had he not had the surgeries, I am convinced that he would eventually have become blind. The gardening that he seemed to be enjoying during our chance encounter would have been an activity of the past. He would not have been able to see the beautiful flowers.

At the time of the ACGME visit, there were only two full-time faculty: Almira and me. But we cobbled together many committed part-time and volunteer faculty. The ACGME liked what they saw and granted us full reaccreditation. I read and reread their letter in my office, breathless. In my heart, though, I knew that we were not yet a good ophthalmology training program. We still had a lot of work to do. I took the ACGME's decision not as an affirmation of program achievement but of the potential of the program to be successful. One of the reviewers mentioned to me that the program reminded him of the motto "I think I can! I think I can!" of the classic children's tale *The Little Engine That Could.* The faculty, residents, and I continued to work hard, and over the next several years the ophthalmology residency garnered the reputation of being one of the best—if not the best—residency program at the KDMC.

Because of the program's success, in 1991, I attracted the attention of the president of Charles Drew, Reed Tuckson, and he asked me to to take over as interim dean of the medical school when the dean was terminated. I agreed to do so but on the condition that I would return to my position as the head of ophthalmology once a permanent dean was recruited. It was a tremendous honor to be asked to become the interim dean, particularly given that I was only thirty-eight years old, but I loved working with the faculty and residents in our ophthalmology program and I wanted to get back to doing what provided me so much joy.

After about a year of being the interim dean, as the search was nearing its end, the search committee recommended to the president that I be hired permanently. I had not sought the position and was ambivalent when the president extended the offer. But he convinced me that academic administration would be rewarding and fun. Thirty years later, I would agree with the rewarding part; I'm still waiting for the fun part.

As dean, I was able to work on a larger scale than as chief of ophthalmology on issues of racial disparity in health and in biomedical training. That, in turn, paved the way for larger administrative roles with even greater impact in academics. These aspects of my career have been immensely rewarding. But I do believe that my time treating patients and being in the trenches with faculty and residents was the most enjoyable.

It is unfortunate that the KDMC was closed in 2007 after federal regulators found that it was unable to meet minimum standards for patient care. I realized then that I had been naive in 1986 when I accepted the position of chief of ophthalmology despite an impending ACGME visit. I had reasoned that the ACGME would not shut down the ophthalmology program because it was too important to the community. After the KDMC was closed, I recognized that the ACGME would have had no qualms about closing down our ophthalmology program had we not met minimal standards, and I now take nothing for granted. If regulators can close down a hospital as important to the community as the KDMC, anything can happen. Along with Howard University, the ophthalmology program there had trained a large proportion of the minority ophthalmologists in the country. Regrettably, there are fewer minority ophthalmologists trained annually now than thirty years ago.

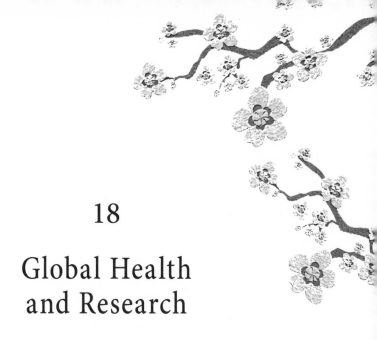

18

Global Health and Research

Because of my interest in different cultures, I dabbled in global health and research during my career. The first time I traveled overseas for something medicine-related was when I went to Oxford for about three or four months to do clinical elective rotations. I began medical school intending to become a psychoanalyst. Along the way, I performed glaucoma-related research and became interested in ophthalmology. But I also had a mild interest in obstetrics and gynecology (ob/gyn) and wanted to explore this specialty further. I decided to explore ob/gyn at Oxford because I would have more of a "hands-on" experience there than at Harvard. Of course, England is a highly developed country and going to Oxford does not really capture the spirit of "global health." Still, I learned a few things while I was there.

In the United Kingdom's educational system, performance on national examinations at an early age determines which educational paths are available to students. The educational pathway to becoming a physician is shorter than in the United States. Specialized courses are taught earlier and students spend less time at the traditional bachelor's degree level. I believe that a longer college education, like that in the United States, is important, as it allows greater time for maturation and for exploring nonmedical interests. I also do not believe the UK system is fair or equitable. Some people are late bloomers and they should not have their educational opportunities limited by how they performed on a test at an earlier stage of life.

I did not notice as much race consciousness in the UK as in the United States, but there was definitely a system of differentiation by social class. A tangible example could be seen in the hospital dining room. The doctors all sat together, the nurses and technical assistants sat together, and other staff sat together. I usually sat with my medical school colleagues but occasionally sat with the nurses or staff, which, as a medical student, was apparently atypical.

My exposure to ob/gyn at Oxford solidified my decision to pursue ophthalmology. Two clinical encounters helped me make this determination. In one of these encounters, I was examining a teenage girl and asked her whether she was sexually active in order to establish a history. This was standard practice; it allowed a physician to determine whether certain tests or prophylactic measures were appropriate. She looked at me for a second and then nonchalantly answered, "No, I just usually lie there." Not sure how to respond, I jotted down, "sexually active" in her history and completed my workup. That was a funny answer, and I can laugh at it now. At the time though, I had to keep composure, and not embarrass the young girl.

The second encounter was witnessed by others and was embarrassing for me. It was 1979 and the sexually suggestive song "Ring My Bell" was number 1 on both the Billboard Hot 100 and the UK Singles Chart. I was performing a pelvic exam on a pregnant woman with the nurse midwife, when all of a sudden, the woman squealed, "Oohh, doctor, you're ringing my bell." Again, I had to maintain composure and finish the exam, but the experience was discomforting. After these experiences, I looked forward to a career examining eyes.

I enjoyed my time at Oxford and occasionally made trips to explore London, which was an hour away by train. Before I left England, I visited R. Pitts Crick, a glaucoma specialist and consultant ophthalmologist at Kings College Hospital in London. Dr. Crick and I had collaborated on a glaucoma database research project, and I brought a draft of the manuscript for review by him. Our paper was published a few years later as the lead article in ophthalmology's premier journal, the *Archives of Ophthalmology*. Titled "Risk Factors for Rate of Progression of Glaucomatous Visual Field Loss," this research collaboration launched my interest in glaucoma and risk factors, two subjects that would form the foundation of my subsequent career.

At that time, "risk factor" was a very new concept. The term was first used in 1961 by investigators conducting the Framingham Heart Study, and most of the references to it were in that context for the next twenty years. In 1980 I conducted a Medline search on the terms "risk factor" or "risk factors" and found that they were used a total of 673 times in all of the medical literature up to that point. I didn't fully comprehend the significance at the time, but my first scientific publication was among the few outside the field of heart disease that studied risk factors. Little did I know that I would be riding an enormous crescendo of a wave as I continued my research on risk factors for glaucoma over the subsequent decades. Thirty-seven years later, I conducted the same Medline search as the one I had done in 1980 and found 73,420 citations. It was serendipity, but my interest and expertise in risk factors for glaucoma were timed perfectly with an explosive growth in the use and understanding of risk factors as a foundational concept in modern-day medicine.

The trip back to the United States was interesting and reinforced my belief in the life-altering potential of higher education. I didn't have enough money to purchase a regular fare air ticket, but there was a place in downtown London that sold steeply discounted tickets on a first-come, first-served basis the day of the flight. I stayed at a colleague's place in London and went every morning until I was finally able to get a ticket I could afford.

There was a girl from the United States who waited every morning also and got a ticket the same time I got mine. We ended up sitting together on the plane. As we were both compatriots trying to get home, she felt comfortable with me and divulged a lot of personal information. After finishing high school, she had gone to Milan, Italy, to model and was currently in transit from Milan. While there, she became pregnant by a well-known NBA basketball player—whose name will remain anonymous—and was now on her way home to face her parents. I recall that she was particularly anxious about seeing her father, who was a general in the military in the Washington, D.C., area.

Her plan was to go home and get an abortion. She wanted to change the trajectory of her life and we discussed the benefits of a college education. She listened intently and asked questions about my alma mater, Allegheny College. Before we landed, she brought up the subject of college again and surprised me by announcing her intent to apply to Allegheny. There was an earnestness to her voice and I believed her.

Years later, I tried to look her up to check on her status. However, the Internet had not yet been invented and I couldn't locate her. I no longer remember her name but hope she went to college, and hope she went to Allegheny. Her attitude was not one of desperation. It was more of a quiet, thoughtful resignation that despite the glamour of high fashion, it was short-lived and would ultimately lead to a dead end. She was at a fork in the road, and she recognized that she needed to take the more difficult path that would lead to greater long-term stability and opportunity. That's what higher education has done for me, and that's why I'm so passionate about it.

After I completed medical school in Boston and my medical internship in New York, I returned to Boston for three years of ophthalmology residency and an additional year of glaucoma fellowship training at the Mass Eye and Ear Infirmary of the Harvard Medical School. It was during this time that I became interested in what would more appropriately be considered global health. The MEEI had worked out an arrangement with the International Eye Foundation (IEF), whose mission was to improve eye health in developing countries, whereby it would send a third-year resident to St. Lucia for six weeks at a time for clinical training supervised by a faculty attending who would stay the full year. The IEF provided partial salary support and a car for the faculty, and the St. Lucian government provided housing for both the faculty and residents as well as the United Kingdom title of consultant ophthalmologist for the faculty. In exchange, we helped train a local St. Lucian primary care physician, Emsco Remy, to become an ophthalmologist and take over ophthalmic care for the island at some future time and took care of patients at the eye clinic of the Queen Victoria Hospital, the main hospital on the island.

My six-week clinical assignment was extraordinarily productive. It was also a great experience from both a clinical and a social perspective. On the clinical side, it offered an opportunity for advanced training and surgery, particularly for glaucoma, which seemed to be very prevalent there. We examined and treated patients who lined up each morning to be seen. Cataract removal and glaucoma surgeries were the most common procedures performed. The number of surgeries we could perform was dependent on how fast we could turn over the operating room between cases. Although electricity was available, it was often unreliable so we always had instruments and machines available for backup that did not require electrical power. We cauterized bleeding with a pointed metal instrument that was heated over an open flame.

With the exception of Tuesdays and Thursdays, when we worked late, as soon as the last patient was seen, I headed for the beach, usually at the St. Lucian Hotel. I did not know how to swim so I learned and became reasonably proficient at it. I also became good friends with the guys who worked at the St. Lucian Hotel in the water sports section. They taught me how to windsurf, and, despite my limited swimming skills, I would venture out into the deep waters. The guys were really nice and thoughtful. Not wanting to embarrass me, they acted as if they weren't paying attention, but I knew they were keeping a very watchful eye, especially Bruno, the head of water sports. Sometimes, when I was struggling with the kite in the water, one of them would nonchalantly come by as if they just happened to be in the area and ask if I needed assistance.

Bruno was the leader and an outstanding windsurfer and water-skier, who once windsurfed from St. Lucia to Martinique, a distance of fifty-one miles. I gravitated toward Joe. Although he knew English, he was more comfortable with patois, the local dialect common in the Caribbean. Joe was shy and didn't talk much, probably because he was self-conscious of his heavy West Indian accent when he spoke English. He was also a bit awkward socially and didn't mingle as much with the other guys who were more sophisticated.

At the end of the day, I often bought them all a round or two of beer and socialized before leaving the beach for home. After a while, I noticed that Joe was always tasked with bringing in the hotel lounge chairs from the beach and could not join us. Feeling bad for him, I began to insist that we wait for Joe to complete his work so that he could join us. Realizing that they could have their beers sooner if they helped Joe bring in the chairs, the other water sports guys pitched in. Joe always appreciated me waiting for him. His mother made delicious chicken rotis that she would sell on the roadside of her home in the nearby fishing village of Gros Islet. Joe always brought me one of her rotis when he knew I would be at the beach.

All of the water sports guys were exceptionally physically fit, muscular without even an ounce of body fat. One day when I was sitting on the beach, I noticed one of them go into his bag, pull out a small bottle, and instill a drop in each eye. I knew that bottle with the yellow label: it was Timolol, a glaucoma medication. I understood from personal experience as a first-year resident a few years earlier that glaucoma can occur in young adults, but I had been taught that it was exceedingly rare. Witnessing this guy, who was younger than me, dropping Timolol into his eyes was a bit of a jolt. I then began to notice that several other glaucoma patients who came to the clinic were young, much younger than the patients with glaucoma I saw in Boston. As will be revealed later, I had a vested interest in better understanding this phenomenon of glaucoma in young Black men, and I resolved to come back to St. Lucia as the faculty attending to further study it.

After my six-week rotation, I began to plan a population-based study of the prevalence of glaucoma on the island, the first such study of glaucoma in a Black population. In addition to developing the study plan, I needed to identify a funding source. Serendipitously, early in my glaucoma fellowship year, I met someone from the United States Agency for International Development (US-AID) after one of our ophthalmology grand rounds on international health, and he mentioned that funding might be available through his organization. There was a catch though: the funding mechanism was only available to HBCUs and Harvard is obviously not an HBCU. For the sole purpose of qualifying for this grant, I obtained a volunteer faculty appointment at Howard University while I was also a glaucoma fellow at the MEEI and brought in Roger Mason, a glaucoma specialist at Howard, to be my co-principal investigator.

With funding for the study secured, I applied for and was selected as the MEEI faculty attending for St. Lucia. During my year there I became well known on the island. This was partly because of my position as the eye doctor for the entire country, and partly because the locals thought I was a bit peculiar.

When I moved to St. Lucia, I had brought a few personal items with me. Among these was a mountain bike, the first one on the island. It was a Peugeot, and I cycled often. The bike was a good way to get to the beach at the St. Lucian Hotel in Rodney Bay. I also sometimes cycled to the clinic in Vieux Fort, which was about forty miles from where I lived, and to the clinic in Soufriere. At about twenty-five miles, Soufriere was not that far, but it was all mountains and the road was narrow and winding. By car, the drive would take at least two hours, and that was if the road conditions were good. It was not that unusual for parts of the road to be impassable, especially after a heavy rain.

I enjoyed cycling to Soufriere. The road hugged the western coastline and I would often stop through the fishing villages of Anse La Raye and Canaries. The fishing boats were all the same style: small and narrow with room for about four or five people. Most just had oars but a few had a rear engine. All were colorful with interesting and creative names written on them. Among my patients were fishermen, who often brought me their fresh catch when they visited the clinic. Invariably, one of them would recognize me when I visited these villages, and we would have a chat before I went along my way. I always remembered Brenda's admonition to me about idealizing their everyday lives. I knew these people and understood the limited career opportunities they faced.

Occasionally, on my way home from Soufriere after an overnight stay, I would cycle along the eastern coastline and go through the villages of Choiseul, Laborie, Micoud, and Dennery, thus completing a loop of the entire island. I didn't have to carry much in the way of food and water. All along the way, the locals would urge me on and provide coconut water and whatever else I needed.

I had intended to carry out the glaucoma study during my year as the MEEI faculty attending on the island. Because of some funding snags with Howard University, however, the study could not begin until the summer of 1986, right as I was leaving for Los Angeles. Fortunately, we were able to hire Sade Kosoko, who had just completed a fellowship in preventive ophthalmology at Johns

Hopkins, to live in St. Lucia and supervise the study. Sade had an interest in epidemiology, and I knew she would do a great job.

I was also glad that Jim Martone, a glaucoma specialist with considerable expertise in international health, succeeded me as the MEEI faculty attending. I had initially met Jim at an annual East Coast vs. West Coast rivalry basketball game at the Association for Research in Vision and Ophthalmology meeting in Sarasota. I thought that he would be outstanding as the faculty attending and had recommended him for the position. He succeeded me, not only as the faculty attending but also on the St. Lucian basketball team, which competed in the Caribbean Regional Championship Tournament.

The subsequent results from the St. Lucia research study, which was published three years after I left the island, were astonishing: the prevalence of glaucoma was four to five times higher than the published prevalence from population-based studies performed in Europe in white populations and it was occurring at an earlier age. Subsequent population-based studies with similar results have now been performed in other Black populations, most notably in Barbados. It is now universally accepted that Blacks have a much higher prevalence of glaucoma than whites and that it often occurs at a younger age.

In early 2001, Sade and I returned to St. Lucia to reexamine the study participants from the initial St. Lucia prevalence study. Sade had gone to Howard University as an ophthalmology resident and had become a member of the glaucoma faculty. In 2000, I had recruited her to Creighton University, where I was the dean of the School of Medicine and vice president of Health Sciences.

What Sade and I found was disturbing. After the conclusion of the initial prevalence survey, the subjects who were identified as having glaucoma were treated by the MEEI ophthalmologists at Queen Victoria Hospital. They were given free glaucoma medications and were treated with surgery when necessary. But after several years, the MEEI presence had discontinued because of safety considerations after one of the female residents was attacked. Ultimately, glaucoma care on the island of St. Lucia became fragmented and inconsistent.

Many patients had discontinued coming to the clinic and were therefore not undergoing treatment for their glaucoma. We found that more than half of the patients showed progression of their visual field loss and at least 16 percent had become blind in at least one eye.* These results were sobering. They offered definitive evidence that untreated glaucoma—or at least suboptimally treated glaucoma—can have disastrous consequences on sight.

～♫ン

Several years after concluding the initial St. Lucia study, I explored funding opportunities to perform another population-based study of glaucoma, this time in Sub-Saharan Africa. I reached out to US-AID since they had funded my St. Lucia study. After extensive discussions, it became obvious that US-AID would not fund another glaucoma prevalence study. However, an intriguing alternative came up during one of my discussions with a project director there.

US-AID had given a contract to an organization called VITAL to perform vitamin A–related studies in Cameroon. The US-AID project director thought that perhaps I could partner with VITAL on a study that could use the same study design to examine the prevalence of vitamin A deficiency in children and of visual impairment and blindness in adults in Cameroon. Vitamin A deficiency can be identified in children by examining the conjunctiva and cornea of the eye. I had wanted to perform a survey of glaucoma but the logistics of transporting visual field machines to remote locations would have been insurmountable. If the study were to be performed, the adult portion of the study would need to be altered to include only basic instrumentation.

If such a study could be organized, the funds provided to VITAL could be maximally leveraged, US-AID could supplement the funding required to perform the adult portion of the study, and the technical expertise of VITAL and my research team could be combined to ensure greater impact.

---

* See R. P. Mason et al., "National Survey of the Prevalence and Risk Factors of Glaucoma in St. Lucia, West Indies," *Ophthalmology* 96, no. 9 (1989): 1363–68; M. Roy Wilson et al., "Progression of Visual Field Loss in Untreated Glaucoma Patients and Glaucoma Suspects in St. Lucia, West Indies," *American Journal of Ophthalmology* 134, no. 3 (2002): 399–405. (A more detailed version of the study in *American Journal of Ophthalmology* was published as a thesis to fulfill a membership requirement for the American Ophthalmological Society.)

After many months of discussions, the collaboration with VITAL was finalized and we began planning in earnest. It was a huge undertaking that required multiple trips to Cameroon to solicit the cooperation of multiple potential partners. The Department of Public Health of Cameroon was obviously the most important partner, and they assigned their chief medical epidemiologist, Amos Sam-Abbenyi, to the project as well as other personnel. Nongovernmental organizations (NGOs) including Save the Children, UNICEF, Sightsavers, and the International Agency for the Prevention of Blindness provided substantial technical assistance and logistical support. One of the NGOs provided four-wheel-drive off-road vehicles that were needed to reach the many remote locations we surveyed. Serge Resnikoff and Dominique Negrel, two highly regarded global health experts from the World Health Organization's Prevent Blindness and Deafness Unit, helped train local physicians, nurses, and technical staff on survey methodology and fieldwork. The sampling strategy and biostatistical expertise was provided by Dennis Ross-Degnan, who worked in the Department of Social Medicine at Harvard Medical School. Mohamed Mansour, the Africa Regional Consultant for the US-AID Office of Nutrition, was the person with whom I primarily worked in planning and implementing the logistical aspects of the study. Mohamed was from Tunisia and spoke several languages, including French, the primary international language used in Cameroon.

It took more than a year of planning. Since the Internet and email were not yet in widespread use, and phone calls were impractical for routine use, we all communicated primarily via fax. In addition to frequent faxes, Mohamed and I traveled to Cameroon about half a dozen times, sometimes separately and sometimes together.

On one of our planning trips, I had arranged for Mohamed and me to meet with the minister of public health of Cameroon at his office in Yaounde, the capital city. When we got there, we were surprised to find that all of the higher-level government officials had gone to a weeklong retreat in the resort town of Kribi, about 175 miles away.

Mohamed and I had traveled long distances to meet with the minister of public health, so we had no choice but to go to Kribi and attempt to meet him there. We rented a car and drove for six hours. Once there, we could not easily find lodging because the government officials had taken all the hotel rooms. We finally found a house that rented rooms, and the following day we were able to meet with the minister at his hotel and fulfill our purpose for traveling to Kribi.

Kribi was not an international tourist destination. It was a resort for Cameroonians, and there were not many international services available. Finding someplace to stay was not the only challenge. Credit cards were not accepted anywhere, and we had no local currency. I've traveled to a lot of places, but never had I been somewhere where even banks would not exchange U.S. dollars for local currency. Fortunately, the owner of the house where we stayed wanted to take us out to dinner that first evening to a traditional Cameroonian restaurant so we at least would have something to eat after the long trip.

To our good fortune, everyone at the restaurant knew our host, among them a man whose daughter wanted to attend school in the United States. We were able to exchange our dollars for local currency with him. Both our housing and money problems were thus solved.

The food was another matter. It was probably tasty but I don't know because I didn't eat. The restaurant had no menus. Everyone just seemed to know what to order. "Would you like some monkey paw?" our host asked in a low whisper. I don't remember Mohamed's response, but mine was a definite no. "They also have some nice snake," she continued. At this point, I thought she was kidding and having fun at our expense. She wasn't; the restaurant lacked menus because it was serving bushmeat. Despite being tired and hungry after a long, stressful day, I went back to my room with my belly empty.

As the preparatory stage was concluding, I had been away from home and my job for months and needed to get back to Los Angeles. I asked Jim Martone, who had succeeded me in St. Lucia as the faculty attending, to travel to Cameroon for what I thought would be fairly routine checks to make sure all arrangements were in place for the survey to begin. Jim was the ideal person for this role as he had been the inaugural medical director for Orbis International, an NGO dedicated to saving sight worldwide, and was accustomed to the challenges of working in a developing world environment.

By now, I had gotten to know Jim closely as I volunteered on Orbis on multiple surgical missions to destinations in the Caribbean, Africa, and Asia. One of our trips together was in Douala, the largest city in Cameroon and its economic capital, so Jim was familiar with the country. Getting him involved was a propitious decision as many of the arrangements I thought had been worked out had to be reestablished and Jim took it all in stride. A person with less experience working in developing country environments would have deemed the situation as hopeless and would have given up.

Cameroon is divided into ten provinces (now called regions). We decided to conduct our survey in the Extreme North Province, the poorest region of the country and the region with the fewest doctors per capita. Life expectancy at the time of the survey was less than fifty years, and there were fewer than two ophthalmologists per million inhabitants. Even that was based on the presence or absence of Medecins Sans Frontieres (Doctors Without Borders); at times, this organization was the sole provider of health care in the region.

After at least a year of planning and months of training the local teams, we conducted the survey of vitamin A deficiency in children five years of age and younger and of visual impairment and blindness in adults in the Extreme North Province of Cameroon.* Two or three teams consisting—at a minimum—of a physician ophthalmologist, nurse, and technician visited each household that had been previously identified and mapped for inclusion in the sample.

Every evening, after returning from the fieldwork, I transferred the data collected onto a laptop. Usually we stayed at a hotel in Maroua, the capital city of the province; sometimes we stayed in Kousseri, a town about 140 miles north of Maroua. A few times, we had to visit villages remote from Maroua and Kousseri. On these occasions, we either had a long drive back to the hotel late at night or we sheltered overnight in a hut provided by the chief of the village surveyed. Once when we were driving back late, the driver stopped and turned

---

* M. Roy Wilson et al., "Prevalence and Causes of Low Vision and Blindness in the Extreme North Province of Cameroon, West Africa," *Ophthalmic Epidemiology* 3, no. 1 (1996): 23–33.

off the headlights for a few minutes. It was so dark that I couldn't even see my hands in front of my face.

Aside from the long days, finding good food was problematic. After seeing flies swarming all over the meat being sold in the outdoor markets, I opted for just cooked vegetables and rice. After more than two months on this diet, I lost more than fifteen pounds.

For the vitamin A portion of the study, we found that the prevalence of its deficiency exceeded the WHO definition of a public health problem.* The good thing about vitamin A deficiency is that it can be cured with a pill. Working with my contacts at the WHO, I was able to get vast quantities of vitamin A pills donated to us by Pfizer, and we treated all the children with signs of vitamin A deficiency. For the adult portion of the study, the data were useful for developing a strategy for a national plan to prevent blindness.

Through Jim, Orbis International got involved after the conclusion of the survey and, together with VITAL, organized a follow-up symposium in Maroua. The purpose of the symposium was to gather ministers of health and other high-level government health officials from Cameroon and neighboring countries to review the survey results. Orbis and VITAL funded this symposium. About forty or so high-level government officials attended.

After the first day of the two-day symposium, a small group of us went to a prearranged dinner on the banks of the River Mayo Kaliao. The river dries up during the dry season and the locals dig in the dry riverbed for water to wash clothes. By word of mouth, we had found a woman who would occasionally cook for small groups. She made us fish—which was only available at a faraway reservoir since the river was dry—and other items for consumption on a picnic table outside her home on the banks of the river.

This was one of the most memorable dinners of my life. There were six of us at the dinner: Jim Martone and Chad MacArthur from Orbis, Peggy from VITAL, a French man who performed the assays for the blood retinol levels, his

---

* M. Roy Wilson et al., "A Population-Based Study of Xerophthalmia in the Extreme North Province of Cameroon, West Africa," *Archives of Ophthalmology* 114, no. 4 (1996): 464–68.

wife, and me. The French couple lived with the Pygmies for part of every year and had developed such a close relationship with them that they were married by them in a traditional ceremony. Jim had been to Albania the week before coming to Cameroon and he brought a bottle of Albanian cognac. The French man rightly claimed that cognac can only come from the Cognac region of France. He refused to even try it. I thought it was curious that someone who was open-minded enough to get married by the Pygmies was not open-minded enough to even try cognac that wasn't from France.

What happened after dinner was even more memorable. It was a beautiful night and we decided to walk the mile or two back to the hotel instead of getting taxis. We were walking at different speeds and after a while Jim and I were well in front of the others and out of sight. At one point, a local man passed us walking in the opposite direction. As he passed, our eyes locked for a moment and he seemed to size us up before continuing to walk. The encounter seemed a bit strange, but I brushed my instincts aside. A few minutes later, we heard a hysterical yell from Peggy. Jim and I ran back to the group and found Peggy and the others acting frantically. The man who had passed us had grabbed Peggy's purse and run off. Peggy was distraught. Her purse was not just any purse. The robber had hit the jackpot. It contained the passports and airline tickets of many of the visiting diplomats as well as several thousand dollars in cash for the per diem payments for all the participants. The hotel did not have a safe and keeping important documents and cash with her was the most prudent thing to do.

Jim and I ran into the alleyway where the man had gone. After about fifty yards, we realized the futility of our chase and stopped. We were in an area that was full of narrow alleyways that branched out in all directions, like a maze. People and livestock were everywhere and on each side were hard-packed dirt walls with an occasional door or gate to living quarters. We were in unfamiliar territory, and it would have been foolhardy to continue. Utterly dejected, we slowly walked back in the direction we had come.

As Jim and I exited the maze toward the group, a jeep jumped the curb and sped across a dirt field in our direction. It screeched to a stop directly in front of us and two Cameroonian men walked out. One of them was carrying Peggy's purse.

They were young, probably in their late twenties, and worked for a local NGO. One of the men, the driver, handed the purse to Peggy. "We saw what happened," he said excitedly. "We knew where he would have to come out from the alley so we waited and jumped him. The guy was so surprised that he dropped the purse."

Peggy was not only relieved; she was absolutely ecstatic. She reached into the purse and pulled out a few hundred-dollar bills for a reward. The two men refused to take it. "We know why you are here," the driver said. "Thank you for what you are doing." The other man added, "We do not want you to have a bad impression of Cameroonians. Not all of us are like that thief."

The per capita income of people in Maroua was about seven hundred dollars. What was in the purse was the equivalent of many years of income. The reward itself was the equivalent of several months of salary for both of these men. Yet they refused to take it because they wanted us to know that not all Cameroonians behaved badly. This experience reinforced for me that there are good people and bad people all over the world. Goodness and badness are not country-specific; they are people-specific.

One such country that has policies that are difficult for me to fully reconcile, but whose people I've found to be wonderful, is Saudi Arabia. I was invited to join the glaucoma faculty at the King Khaled Eye Specialist Hospital (KKESH) in Riyadh for a few months in the early 1990s. I jumped at the opportunity as I had heard rumors of a high prevalence of childhood glaucoma among the nomadic Arab, or Bedouin, population and I would be able to witness it for myself.

I had been studying the efficacy and safety of a new glaucoma implant called the Ahmed Glaucoma Valve Implant.* Glaucoma implants were fairly new, and this one had some theoretical advantages to the other ones available

---

* A. L. Coleman et al., "Initial Clinical Experience with the Ahmed Glaucoma Valve Implant in Pediatric Patients," *American Journal of Ophthalmology* 120, no. 1 (1995): 23–31; A. L. Coleman et al., "Clinical Experience with the Ahmed Glaucoma Valve Implant in Eyes with Prior or Concurrent Penetrating Keratoplasties," *American Journal of Ophthalmology* 123, no. 1 (1997): 54–61.

at the time. Implants have a tube that penetrates into the anterior chamber of the eye. Aqueous fluid drains through the tube into the body of the implant and is then distributed into the conjunctiva posteriorly. The main challenge with implants was that it was difficult to control how much fluid was drained from the eye. If too much was drained, the intraocular pressure became dangerously low and could cause significant complications.

The Ahmed Glaucoma Valve Implant had a valve mechanism that would theoretically close off the fluid flow when the intraocular pressure got too low. I thought that it might be useful for the pediatric population, particularly when follow-up might be limited, as would be the case with the nomadic Bedouins; I brought a large supply of these implants with me.

The Ahmed implant was a big hit. The glaucoma faculty at KKESH were not using implants very often, but whatever implant they were using was completely replaced by the Ahmed implant. Also, glaucoma implants generally were rarely used in the pediatric population because of the amount of follow-up needed. If the intraocular pressure got too low because of excess drainage of fluid, unlike in the adult population, intervention would require general anesthesia, which had its risks. The valve mechanism with the Ahmed implant enabled it to be used in children with greater confidence.

One of the kids I operated on with the Ahmed implant was the son of a prominent Saudi gentleman. He was very close to the royal family and reportedly had dinner with the king of Saudi Arabia, Fahd I, on a weekly basis. In appreciation, he invited me to his sprawling compound and had a huge feast prepared in my honor. All of the meat, including goat and lamb, as well as some more exotic meats, was fresh from his grounds. About a hundred people attended, all the men in one tent and women in another.

During my time at KKESH, I met some wonderful people, many of whom I still consider friends. Each subspecialty at KKESH had both an expat from the United States and a local Saudi as its leaders. The expat head was David Dueker, who was my mentor at the MEEI. The local head was Ibrahim Jadaan. At the time, Ibrahim was a relatively inexperienced ophthalmologist. I've enjoyed watching him develop into a seasoned, and terrific, glaucoma specialist.

Since that time at KKESH, I have traveled to Saudi Arabia six or seven times, usually to Jeddah, and usually to develop collaborations between my university, the University of Colorado Denver, and Saudi universities. On most of these trips, my host was Zuhair Fayez, a prominent architect/developer and alumnus of the University of Colorado. He was the founder of Dar Al-Hekma University, a private, nonprofit institution of higher education for women. One of the collaborations I established was between Dar Al-Hekma and the College of Architecture and Planning at the University of Colorado Denver.

Zuhair was always a gracious host and we became friends. I was invited to the marriage celebration of one of his daughters in Jeddah. It was a lavish event with over a thousand guests in a huge private tent. Cars drove through one side of the tent that had a private entryway secluded from view and let people off. Once inside, women abandoned their traditional abaya (long black cloak that covers all but the hands and face) and displayed gorgeous designer gowns and jewels. The temporary bathrooms were like those you would encounter at the Four Seasons Hotel with porcelain bowls and gold-plated faucets. Zuhair had several homes around the globe, including in London and Aspen. Aside from his daughter's best friend, who was from Aspen, I was the only non-Saudi person there.

On my way home from KKESH on my initial Saudi Arabia trip, I took a detour to visit Professor Upali Mendis in Sri Lanka. I flew first class but made the mistake of traveling on an airline that prohibited alcohol. After months without wine, I had been looking forward to a nice glass with dinner.

The largest inpatient eye hospital in the world is in Colombo, Sri Lanka, and Dr. Mendis was in charge. It was the first of several trips I would make to Sri Lanka as we became friends and collaborators. Dr. Mendis headed up the Sri Lanka site for an international clinical trial I conducted several years later comparing the Ahmed implant to standard trabeculectomy surgery in the surgical treatment of glaucoma.[*] The other international site was KKESH in Saudi Arabia.

---

[*] M. Roy Wilson et al., "Ahmed Glaucoma Valve Implant vs Trabeculectomy in the Surgical Treatment of Glaucoma," *American Journal of Ophthalmology* 130, no. 3 (2000): 267–73.

In 1995, I was invited to deliver the University Lecture at the University of Colombo. This named lectureship was not in ophthalmology or even in medicine. It was a lectureship for the entire university, and it was a great privilege for me to deliver it.

One of the greatest honors in the field of medicine is election to the National Academy of Medicine (NAM), of which there are twelve sections representing different disciplines in medicine. Section 12, Administration of Health Services, Education, and Research, is for those who have made significant contributions to medicine through administrative work such as being a dean of a medical school, president of an academic medical center, or president of a national medical organization. Many administrative leaders who are members of NAM were elected through this section. Although my career in administrative leadership would have qualified me for election through Section 12 also, I feel particularly proud to have been elected to NAM through the section related to my academic area of focus, Section 06, Surgery, Anesthesiology, Radiology, Ophthalmology. When my election was formally announced, my administrative career was not mentioned in the citation; it focused exclusively on contributions made to medicine through glaucoma epidemiology and global health.

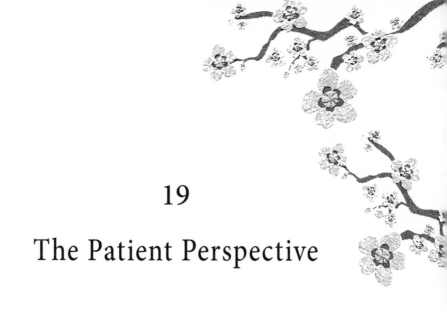

19

The Patient Perspective

For much of my life, my identity was based on my physical and mental strength. I certainly had my share of athletic injuries, but I always played through pain. During track practice in junior high school, I walked into the path of a shot put and got hit in the head about an inch above my temple. It knocked me out for a while, but I refused to go to the hospital. I also played an entire game of varsity soccer that year with a sore toe that was later diagnosed as broken. Playing football in high school, I was hit in the rib cage with such force that I heard a crack and had the wind knocked out of me. I protected that side of the body with my arms and played on despite excruciating pain from simply breathing.

I often felt like I was invincible, and not just physically. Because of my childhood experience of growing up alone, I also believed that I could survive on my own whatever the circumstances. I shunned any sort of dependence.

The first chink in my armor occurred when I was diagnosed with glaucoma at the young age of twenty-eight. How could this be? I was a first-year ophthalmology resident and glaucoma was considered a disease of old age.

The diagnosis came about due to the fight I had instigated at the sandwich shop after the employee put mayo on my sandwich. One of my resident colleagues who treated me in the MEEI emergency room recommended I be seen at the clinic where I worked the following day. It wasn't a formal appointment. During a lull in the schedule, I went over to one of the adjacent exam lanes and asked one of the senior residents, Frank Spellman, to examine me.

Frank was only the second or third Black resident to be trained at the MEEI. His father, Dr. Mitch Spellman, was a pioneering surgeon with a very distinguished career. Among other posts, Mitch Spellman was founding dean of the Charles Drew Postgraduate Medical School—later renamed the Charles Drew University of Medicine and Science, the institution where I would later serve as dean of the medical school, president of the university, and chair of the governing board—and dean for medical services at Harvard Medical School.

Frank was an outstanding ophthalmology resident as well as a friend. He examined me at the slit lamp between his regularly scheduled patients and diagnosed iritis (inflammation in the anterior chamber of the eye) as well as a bit of a hyphemia (blood in the anterior chamber) in the eye that was punched. He also noticed that the intraocular pressure (IOP) in both eyes was elevated. Typically, IOP should be below 21 mmHg; mine was in the range of 35 mmHg. Although inflammation in the eye can cause an elevation of IOP, it seemed odd that the IOP was elevated in both eyes, and Frank insisted on dilating my pupils to take a good look at my optic nerves.

The optic nerve (or optic disc) is made of a central cup surrounded by neural tissue. The ratio of the cup to the entire disc is typically in the range of 0.3 or 0.4 but is increased in glaucoma. My cup-disc ratio was in the range of 0.8 to 0.9 in both eyes, indicating that I had lost neural tissue. As Frank had suspected, my IOP was elevated because of glaucoma and not because of the inflammation in the injured eye.

Sitting in the chair in his examination lane, I could hardly believe my diagnosis. As an ophthalmology resident I examined many patients with glaucoma; all were old and most were visually handicapped or blind. He saw a silver lining though: "You know, Roy, if you hadn't sustained an eye injury, it's likely that your first eye exam wouldn't have occurred until middle age when we check for reading glasses. You would have been close to blind by then." His statement was based on sound medical rationale, but it didn't make me feel much better.

Over the next several weeks, the inflammation in my eye subsided and my IOP was reduced by eye drop medications. I never had a formal clinic visit, there was never an official record of my diagnosis, and Frank never divulged my diagnosis to anyone (except possibly his wife). As an ophthalmology resident, I had access to the necessary medications and I self-treated. The ophthalmic photographer, Audrey, was a good friend and she knew about my diagnosis. She took pictures of my optic nerves periodically so that I could monitor for progressive cupping.

The other piece of data necessary for monitoring potential progression is the visual field. During this time, automated visual field machines were being introduced, and these automated perimeters did not require a technician to manually perform the exam as was the case with the traditional Goldman perimeter. Having access to the locked clinics during off-hours, I performed my own visual fields with one of these new automated machines at periodic intervals.

Why did I go through such efforts to hide my diagnosis? Perhaps I feared that public knowledge of my having a potentially blinding disease might influence people's perception of me as an ophthalmologist and might negatively impact my career. Part of it, though, was that I felt vulnerable and did not want people to see me that way. *No chinks in the armor!*

For years I struggled with the glaucoma eye drops. The primary glaucoma medication at the time was Timolol, the same eye drop I would see the young guy using at the beach in St. Lucia a few years later. Timolol is in a class of medications called beta blockers, and beta blockers work by slowing the heart rate. When taken orally, it is used to treat certain heart conditions. As an eye drop, the amount absorbed systemically is low and most people are not affected by the heart rate slowing by just a few beats per minute. However, I was very active, playing basketball, running, and cycling, and I could tell that the Timolol was affecting my ability to get my heart rate up to peak performance levels. Additionally, beta blockers cause the airways in the lungs to contract, making it difficult to breathe for those prone to asthma. I had mild asthma as a child and occasionally noticed a recurrence of wheezing after physical exertion, which I attributed to the Timolol. I didn't like the medication, but it was the best drug available for glaucoma at the time, so I tolerated it.

Since my IOP was still too elevated, I also started taking pilocarpine hydrochloride eye drops, which had minimal systemic side effects but a lot of ocular side effects. As we age, the ability of the eye to change its focus from distant to near objects (and vice versa), a process called accommodation, is lost. Accommodation occurs through the crystalline lens changing shape, and the lens loses that ability as we age. That is why we need reading glasses when we get older. Pilocarpine causes the lens to change shape and accommodation to occur. In older people who can no longer accommodate, pilocarpine is well tolerated; in young people, the forced accommodation causes blurry vision and brow aches. For me, these side effects were intolerable.

In the late 1970s, an ophthalmic insert with pilocarpine in it was introduced. It consisted of a membrane device that was inserted under the upper lid. The drug was supposed to be released continuously at a controlled rate through the membrane into the tear fluid and thereby reduce the intensity of the side effects. Another advantage of the insert, called Ocusert Pilo, was that each one lasted for seven days.

It didn't work for me. The drug was supposed to be released in a controlled, sustained way, but I found that it would release in spurts and cause intense brow aches and nearsightedness at inopportune times. More than once I had to pull off to the side of the road while driving because I couldn't see beyond the steering wheel. Also, the insert would move around under the lid and sometimes float down over the cornea. Not only was this uncomfortable, but it was difficult to explain it to people who noticed.

Another common class of medication at the time was ophthalmic epinephrine. As with pilocarpine hydrochloride, systemic side effects were uncommon but ocular side effects were very common and included hypersensitivity, chronic irritation, and hyperemia (redness of the eye). Dipivefrin (Propine), a prodrug of epinephrine, was able to achieve better corneal penetration and had been reported to produce even fewer systemic side effects, but it still had a high incidence of ocular side effects.

My glaucoma drug regimen for many years was Timolol and Propine. Although my IOP was much lower than pretreatment, I did not consider it optimal. As a glaucoma specialist, I understood glaucoma's toll on sight and on the lives of those burdened with the disease. It was a time of great anxiety as I fretted about the possibility of becoming blind.

Then, in 1996, a new class of medication, a prostaglandin-based drug called latanoprost (Xalatan), was introduced by Pharmacia. I switched out the Propine for Xalatan, and the result was remarkable—my IOP was reduced to the low teens. In 2002, I joined the Faculty Advisory Board of Pharmacia (later Pfizer, which bought out Pharmacia in 2003). This enabled me to have access to prepublication Xalatan research data as well as the clinical wisdom of some of the leading glaucoma specialists in the country. And because I had a personal stake in the drug, I devoted a lot of time and energy to my advisory role. Eventually, I discontinued the Timolol and used Xalatan alone with great IOP control.

I am fortunate. Now, forty years after my diagnosis, I've experienced minimal, if any, progression of the disease, my optic nerve cupping has been remarkably stable, and my visual fields are practically normal. This is not the normal course for the disease, and I am thankful. However, I had no way of predicting my stable glaucoma course, and knowing that I had a potentially blinding disease at such a young age has had a profound impact on my life.

After I conducted the population-based study on glaucoma in St. Lucia, I feared that I would likely become blind, or at least severely visually handicapped, at some point during my career as an ophthalmologist. I consequently decided to pursue formal training in epidemiology and seek administrative opportunities in medicine in case my career as an ophthalmic surgeon was compromised by poor sight.

In 1989, while working as chief of ophthalmology at the King/Drew Medical Center and as a glaucoma faculty member at the Jules Stein Eye Institute of UCLA, I enrolled to obtain a master of science degree in epidemiology at UCLA's School of Public Health and received my degree a year later. A few years later, in 1993, I more earnestly pursued my administrative career, initially as dean of the medical school at the Charles R. Drew University of Medicine and Science and associate dean at the UCLA School of Medicine. Both decisions have proved to be auspicious. My extra training in epidemiology put me on a course to become a prominent ophthalmic epidemiologist, particularly as it relates to glaucoma; and my early administrative forays paved the path for leadership at the very highest levels of both medical schools and universities.

I currently have perfect 20/15 vision (better than the commonly used 20/20 benchmark), and my need for a backup plan in epidemiology or administration did not materialize. My career as an academic clinician taking care of glaucoma patients has been extraordinarily rewarding and I could have continued doing that for my entire career. Yet, epidemiology offered an opportunity for me to distinguish myself as an academic, and I doubt that I would have progressed through the professorial ranks as rapidly without the extra training. As for academic administration, I recall a conversation many years ago with my son, Yoshio, when he was still a young boy and I was dean of a medical school. He lamented, "Dad, you used to fix people's eyes and make them better; now, all you do is sit behind a desk and push paper." I explained that I still helped people but that it was through policy changes that impacted large groups of people rather than through one-on-one interactions. I loved fixing people's eyes, but I know that academic administration has provided me an opportunity to impact the lives of many more people.

Knowing what I now know as a glaucoma specialist, it is difficult to explain why my glaucoma had not progressed. Because I wanted to keep my diagnosis a secret, I never had a formal clinical exam and never had my health insurance cover any glaucoma-related expenses. Rather, I managed my own disease, finding ways to get my intraocular pressure checked and optic nerve photos and visual fields taken.

After twenty-two years, in 2003, I decided to entrust my glaucoma care to someone else and methodically went through the process of selecting that person. Obviously, I personally knew glaucoma specialists with the best academic reputations in the world, and many were close friends. But I had specific criteria for selection that were of importance to me. I wanted a glaucoma clinician who had their own private practice office rather than someone in a university-based academic practice. A university-based practice would have more billing and scheduling restraints that could compromise my identity. And although I am very supportive of medical training, having trainees involved in my care—as would be the case in a university-based clinic—would also increase the risk of having my identity exposed. Most of the world-renowned glaucoma specialists I personally knew were in university-based practices.

Believing that I might need surgery at some point, my main criterion for selection was reputation as an outstanding surgeon. As a surgeon myself, the thought of undergoing eye surgery was oddly frightening. Selecting a surgeon to operate on my eyes was not a trivial matter and I had very strong views on what it meant to be an outstanding surgeon. These views were shaped early, during my first year of ophthalmology training.

Two presentations greatly influenced me at the 1981 meeting of the New England Ophthalmological Society (NEOS). One was a debate between two highly regarded ophthalmologists on whether cataracts should be removed using an extracapsular technique (ECCE) or intracapsular technique (ICCE). ICCE involves the removal of the lens and surrounding capsule in one piece and was the favored form of cataract extraction from the late 1960s to the early 1980s. People wearing thick "coke bottle" type glasses had this procedure performed. In ECCE, the lens capsule in the front of the lens is removed and the lens nucleus is removed through the opening. There actually is no debate. ECCE is far superior—an analogy might be a Ferrari to a Pinto—and has been used exclusively now for decades, even in developing countries. Yet, here was this famous ophthalmologist trying to argue for ICCE. I realized that some people are simply resistant to change, no matter the evidence in favor of it.

The other presentation was one in which I learned about phacoemulsification cataract surgery, which is an extracapsular technique in which the lens nucleus is emulsified with an ultrasonic handpiece and aspirated from the eye. This is how modern-day cataract surgery is performed worldwide. I did not learn phacoemulsification during my residency or fellowship training. It was considered too avant-garde by many of the professors at the MEEI.

The change from ICCE to ECCE and the advent of phacoemulsification have proved to be the two most significant advances—actually quantum leaps—in cataract surgery. Glaucoma surgery, on the other hand, had not advanced at all since the trabeculectomy procedure was introduced in 1968. However, a new procedure, micro-invasive glaucoma surgery (MIGS), was beginning to take hold in some glaucoma circles, and I thought it seemed promising. Remembering the lessons learned at the 1981 NEOS meeting, I wanted a technically skilled surgeon who was innovative and who was experienced in this new method in case it turned out to be the right procedure for me. MIGS was a safer procedure and therefore allowed surgical intervention at a much earlier course of the disease. Though it didn't produce the same level of IOP lowering as a trabeculectomy, I at least wanted it as an option if I needed to have surgery.

After careful consideration, I asked Ron Fellman of Dallas to be my ophthalmologist. Ron had a reputation as an innovative surgeon with good hands, and he had his own practice. Additionally, he was academically inclined, and we both attended and presented at many of the same glaucoma specialty meetings. I felt comfortable with him, and he started taking care of my glaucoma.

Understanding my desire to keep my diagnosis private, he never charged my health insurance for the visits. He could have charged me out of pocket but didn't. In appreciation, I always flew to Dallas a day early and took him and his wife, Nancy, to dinner the evening before my appointments. Prior to 2003, I knew Ron from the various meetings we both attended and had high regard for him, but I would not have considered him a friend. Both Ron and Nancy are now good friends, and I have come to know one of their daughters, Melissa, as well. Melissa wanted to be a physician and I occasionally saw her as a young girl accompanying her dad in the clinic. After medical school, she pursued neurology training at the University of Miami Health System and then stayed on as a junior faculty member. I now sit on the Board of Directors of the University of Miami Health System, and when I spot her around the hospital I'm reminded of how long I've been her father's patient.

I mentioned earlier that my visual fields are near normal. My field defect is only in one eye and it is almost undetectable with the standard visual field protocol that measures the central field out to 24 degrees from center. By extending the test to measure out to 30 degrees from center, the defect is more noticeable. This defect in one eye, more clearly demonstrable using a testing strategy rarely used in clinical practice, is the extent of my visual field loss, and it has remained essentially stable during the entire nineteen years of seeing Ron.

Although he had never examined me, my good friend Bob Weinreb, a brilliant academic glaucoma specialist who knew of my glaucoma history and course, once remarked, "It's really unusual for glaucoma to be so stable over so many years. I've never seen it. I'm not sure that what you have is glaucoma." I do have glaucoma, but I am indeed fortunate.

I dealt with an equally traumatic health issue the year after my glaucoma diagnosis, when I was a second-year resident at the MEEI. One night, while at home, I fainted for no apparent reason, except that I stood up quickly from a prone position. The following morning, on my way to the MEEI, I stopped by the emergency room of the Beth Israel Hospital—a Harvard-affiliated hospital where I had performed many of my clinical rotations as a medical student—for a quick checkup.

After I explained my fainting spell to the emergency room doctor, a full workup was performed, including an electrocardiogram (EKG), which came back abnormal, showing signs of inferolateral Q waves consistent with a myocardial infarction. In simple language, it showed signs of my having had a heart attack. Even though I was feeling perfectly fine, the doctor was very concerned and admitted me to the hospital.

Once I was admitted, my bloodwork ruled out a heart attack as the cause of my fainting, although it could not rule out that I had had a heart attack at some time in the past. I was taken care of by a medical resident who was supervised by a faculty attending. By chance, the faculty attending was someone who had special interest and expertise in cardiomyopathies; he decided that the abnormal EKG was a result of hypertrophic cardiomyopathy.

Cardiomyopathy is a disease of the heart muscle that makes it harder for the heart to pump blood to the rest of the body. Hypertrophic cardiomyopathy involves abnormal thickening of the heart muscle, particularly affecting the left ventricle, which is the main pumping chamber. Because of the faculty attending's interest in cardiomyopathies, I stayed in the hospital for much longer than necessary while all types of esoteric tests were performed.

After about a week, I was discharged. Although I had just wanted a quick checkup, I now had a medical record with a diagnosis of a cardiomyopathy. Unfortunately, I had let my life insurance from John Hancock lapse and could not get it renewed because I was considered "high risk." Despite multiple attempts to get my insurance reinstated, the information in the discharge document painted a picture of someone at high risk of cardiac death, and no amount of pleading on my part was able to sway the insurance underwriters that I was worth the risk.

As a physician, and also from personal experience, I understood the insurance company's rationale for not providing me life insurance. Cardiomyopathy with ventricular hypertrophy had recently been recognized as the most common cause of sudden cardiac death in athletes. I had personally witnessed two sudden deaths attributed to it. In both cases, the arrest was caused by a cardiac arrhythmia, presumably due to left ventricular cardiomyopathy.

The first happened on the playground in D.C. when I was in high school. "J" was the best playground baller I had ever played against—and I played against several who became professional ball players. He had gone to the bathroom between games and after he didn't come out, a few of us went to get him. We found him slumped on the floor and unresponsive. The same thing happened several years later in college. One of the junior varsity players was not feeling well during practice and went to the bathroom. He was also found unresponsive and attempts at resuscitation were unsuccessful.

Having had these experiences, I was not naive and did not take my diagnosis lightly. Several years after my diagnosis, I was introduced socially to a cardiologist who specialized in evaluating athletes and military recruits and I recounted my story. He suspected that instead of cardiomyopathy I had a large muscular left ventricle, a condition he noticed often in his specialized practice and one that can cause the type of variation noted on my EKG. At his invitation, I consulted with him in his office. His diagnosis was that I had a large but normal left ventricle.

Over the years, whenever I made a job-related move, I saw a new primary care doctor. Each time, the new doctor would get anxious about my "abnormal" EKG and would insist that I undergo additional cardiac workup including a stress test and echocardiogram. The stress test always indicated that I had exceptional exercise capacity without undue stress on the heart, and the echocardiogram showed normal functioning without signs of a prior heart attack. I've probably had more cardiac exams than any asymptomatic person has ever had. It is also an indictment on our health care system that I had to get retested every time I moved rather than having a record that was easily accessible to new health care providers.

After approximately ten years postdiagnosis, I shopped around for a life insurance policy. I knew I would be disqualified if the application asked if I had previously ever been denied insurance for medical reasons. I found an application that asked this question but qualified it by adding "within the past seven years." I could honestly answer "no" and was finally able to get life insurance coverage. Ironically, it was with John Hancock.

I got the life insurance because it was the prudent thing to do, regardless of the presence or absence of any medical condition, and not because I was overly concerned with my cardiovascular health. My cardiovascular fitness has repeatedly been evaluated and I've always scored in the superior or elite category, testing in the top 1 percent for my age category in most of the usual metrics. I received the EKG that led to an erroneous diagnosis of hypertrophic cardiomyopathy because I fainted. I've had subsequent fainting spells, almost always after strenuous cycling. I now know that my fainting is caused by a condition called orthostatic hypotension, a sudden drop in blood pressure upon standing from a seated or prone (lying down) position. In my case, I tend to lose a lot of salt in my sweat and get dehydrated after long, strenuous exertion such as long-distance cycling or jogging. The dehydration predisposes my blood pressure to drop upon standing, and the decrease in blood being pumped to my brain causes the fainting. To protect against this happening, I need to take in a lot of salt and water, particularly during long-duration exercise, and be cautious about suddenly standing after exercise. I wish I had known this forty years ago.

My most significant health challenge occurred more recently. In January 2013, I saw a primary care doctor for a routine physical exam. I was fifty-nine years old at the time, and part of a routine physical for a male of that age often includes obtaining a blood PSA (prostate-specific antigen) level. Prostate screening with a PSA level is not without some level of controversy, however, and some physicians recommend against that practice. I was in the camp that did not believe in routine PSA screening. Fortunately, my doctor convinced me to have my PSA level checked. For a man of my age, a PSA level greater than 4 ng/mL is considered abnormal; mine was over 30 ng/mL.

A biopsy performed at MedStar Georgetown University Hospital confirmed that I had advanced prostate cancer.

The next step was to determine if I had metastatic disease, that is, a cancer that has spread to other parts of the body. While a CT scan of the abdomen and pelvis did not show evidence of metastatic disease, a nuclear medicine full-body bone scan showed a focus of activity involving the right tenth rib, and this was determined to be a possible metastasis.

I was deputy director of the National Institute on Minority Health and Health Disparities (NIMHD) of the NIH at the time. Because of the extraordinary resources and expertise at the NIH, I had the biopsy slides sent to Dr. William Dahut, the Scientific Director for Clinical Research at the National Cancer Institute and the head of the Prostate Cancer Clinic. Dr. Dahut had the surgical pathology lab at the NIH interpret the slides, and the initial reading was confirmed. Next, he repeated the bone scan with a highly sensitive 18F sodium fluoride PET/CT scan and performed a high field magnetic resonance (MR) spectroscopy. Both of these tests were very advanced and were not available in most medical centers.

Because of residual blood from the biopsy, the MR spectroscopy result was inconclusive. The bone scan confirmed the lesion noted previously on the right tenth rib; it also picked up lesions on the right ilium (uppermost part of the hip bone) and right skull. The radiologist interpreted these abnormalities as "suggestive for bone metastasis." Dr. Dahut sent the scans to the head radiologist for a second opinion, and he concurred that the lesions in the right ilium and right rib were suspicious for metastatic cancer.

Dr. Dahut forwarded both radiologists' reports to me. It was one thing to be told what the radiologists believed but yet another to actually see it in writing. The evidence pointed toward having metastatic disease (stage 4). One cancer physician with whom I informally consulted thought that someone with the "hypothetical" clinical picture I presented to him could expect to live as little as six months. A review of the available literature led me to believe that his assessment was much too pessimistic and that up to five years was more likely. Still, I was devastated. I felt that I had so much unfinished business, both personally and professionally, and not enough time left.

Dr. Dahut recommended that I be seen in the Prostate Cancer Clinic, where my potential treatment would be discussed by a team of specialists representing various disciplines, including radiology, pathology, surgery, and oncology. But on the day of the appointment, I stopped at the door of the clinic. I saw anxious looks on the faces of the patients as they waited to be seen, and my legs wouldn't move. I could not go in.

It was rumored that one of the NIH leaders I worked with had prostate cancer. He had been seen in the waiting room of that same clinic several weeks earlier by a NIH staff person and everyone was whispering about it. I had what I believed was a terminal illness and desired privacy. Word of my health situation would most certainly have gotten around the NIH had I set foot in that clinic. I called Dr. Dahut later and explained why I had not kept my appointment.

The next day, I received a call from Dr. Dahut, and he asked me to come to a specific conference room at a specific time later in the day. I was met there by Dr. Dahut and a team of about four or five other senior specialist physicians. He had assembled an all-star team to go over my case in the privacy of the conference room.

During the meeting, they projected images of my bone scan, MRI, CT scan, and other tests and discussed each in detail. Consensus was beginning to form that perhaps the suspicious findings noted with the very sensitive bone scan may have been due to past trauma rather than metastatic lesions. When asked if I had ever sustained a rib injury, I recounted my high school football injury. When asked about a head injury, I recounted the episode of being knocked out with a shot put during track and field practice in Japan. With regard to the right ilium lesion, I once had a bicycle accident on Pacific Coast Highway in Malibu in which I flew over my handlebar and landed on my hip. Although I didn't think that my injuries were that severe, I fell with enough force that my helmet was cracked, my bike was trashed, and I had difficulty walking without pain in my hip. After a lot of questions and a lot of discussion, Dr. Dahut finally commented, "We don't think you have metastatic disease. All of these lesions we see are explainable by injuries you've sustained."

From believing that I had metastatic disease and a short time to live, I was now being told that all my abnormal scan findings were explainable by the various athletic injuries I had sustained. It would be difficult to describe the emotional release I felt at that moment. Welling up with tears, I thanked everyone and quickly exited the room, as if staying might cause them to change their minds.

Believing I had only a short time left to live had forced me to reflect deeply on how best to spend whatever time I had in the most meaningful way, reflections that continued to influence me even after it was determined that I didn't have metastatic disease. Remembering my own childhood, I resolved to not repeat my dad's mistakes. Foremost on my mind was that I needed to make sure that Yoshio and Presley felt my love for them. I also needed to let my friends know how important they were to me.

I felt that I was being provided extra years of life to fulfill some purpose. It made me think about a comment that Ms. Stephan once made when she was pushing me to delve deeper into a subject than would have been expected for a high school student. When I balked, she chided, "Roy, you have a unique combination of gifts. Use them and make our society better."

The ensuing three months were arguably the most consequential of my life. I consulted with several prostate specialists on treatment options and vacillated between surgery and radiation. The surgical oncologists invariably recommended surgery and the radiation oncologists always recommended radiation. I asked Dr. Dahut for his opinion. Because the MR spectroscopy could not rule out extracapsular extension—because of the clotted blood from the biopsy—he felt that radiation was the safer option.

After doing some research on radiation therapies, I decided on stereotactic body radiation therapy (SBRT) with CyberKnife. SBRT is an image-guided technique of delivering high doses of radiation to the cancer cells with accuracy while limiting damage to healthy tissues and organs. CyberKnife was a new machine that delivered SBRT; although it contains the word "knife," there is no knife or incision.

By coincidence, Dr. Sean Collins, the radiation oncologist to whom I was referred by the urologist, was an expert on CyberKnife. He works at the Lombardi Comprehensive Cancer Center of Georgetown University Hospital, which fortunately is not far from the NIH. I commenced treatment with CyberKnife (three treatments) and intensity modulated radiation therapy (IMRT, twenty-four treatments). IMRT is an external beam treatment that uses a computer-driven machine that moves around the patient as it delivers radiation. Like the CyberKnife, precise mapping of the prostate lessens the likelihood of damage to surrounding normal tissues and organs.

I started treatment on April 23, 2013. Dr. Collins kindly scheduled me at 7:30 a.m. every day, the first radiation appointment of the day. My girlfriend (now wife) Jacqueline drove me every morning, waited for the treatment session to conclude, and then drove me to my office at the NIH. I would be at my office by 9:00 a.m. and no one, not even my secretary, knew I was being treated for prostate cancer.

In addition to the radiation, I was also given adjuvant hormone therapy (Lupron Depot). The combination of radiation treatment and the hormone caused fatigue. I tried to keep up my exercise regimen, but it was difficult. I was exhausted after lifting just twenty-five-pound weights for barbell back rows (about half of the typical weight for me) and could not walk on the treadmill for more than fifteen minutes. I kept at my exercise, though, because the hormone also caused ten pounds of weight gain, and I needed to burn some calories.

During these three months, from late April to late June, I was contemplating making a career move. I loved being at the NIH for a number of reasons, but I also missed interacting with students and the cadence of university work. About a week before my initial radiation treatment, I had interviewed for the presidency of Wayne State University. My second interview was a month later, and I was offered the position at the end of May. A couple of days after my last radiation session, I visited the Wayne State campus for a public announcement of my appointment at a scheduled meeting of our governing board. The following week, I packed up to move to Detroit.

On my final visit with Dr. Collins before leaving for Detroit, we discussed the impact of the cancer diagnosis on my life. A comment Dr. Collins made resonated with me and I contemplate it often. "I think this experience with cancer will make you a better university president," he said. I don't know if he was correct or not. But I do know that I've gained a deeper perspective on life and on my role in medicine and higher education.

I officially became the twelfth president of Wayne State University on August 1, 2013. No one knew that I had just undergone radiation treatment for prostate cancer and that I was still undergoing hormone therapy. It was important that I kept this information private because of whom I was replacing. Allan Gilmour had been vice-chairman and CFO of the Ford Motor Company and was highly regarded in Michigan. Allan had retired from Ford twice and was financially stable. He did not need the job as president of Wayne State; he did it because he cared and wanted to make a difference.

Allan served for about three years. During the latter half of his presidency, he was diagnosed with prostate cancer and underwent hormone therapy and radiation. Unlike me, he was very public about his diagnosis and its impact on his life. Allan was often fatigued and could not devote his full energies to his very demanding job. In fact, because he was often not feeling well, the board created a new position of deputy president and appointed Phyllis Vroom to that position to deal with the day-to-day responsibilities of the presidency. Given this history, I doubt I would have been selected as the next president had my diagnosis been known; once in my position, I would not have been provided an unbiased opportunity to perform my job.

By the time I began my duties as president on August 1, my energy had returned to normal or near normal, and I projected an image of strength and vigor. I began working out with weights twice a week with a trainer at the university's fitness center and did cardiovascular exercises three or four times a week. The following year, I began cycling again. However, I developed hematuria (blood in the urine), which was attributed to cystitis (inflammation of the bladder). Although cystitis can occur after radiation treatment, it typically does not occur after the first few months post-treatment. On the other hand, my physicians had not treated a patient who cycled anything close to the distances I was cycling so my bladder issues were ultimately attributed to the cycling. I'm an avid cyclist and even did a little racing when I was younger, and the prospect of not being able to cycle because of the cystitis was depressing.

Unbeknownst to me, my wife, Jacqueline, had started researching recumbent bicycles—which would not cause the same pressure on my prostate and bladder—and presented me with some options to consider. After my initial reluctance, at her urging, we traveled to Los Angeles to check out a bicycle shop that specializes in recumbents (Bent-Up Cycles). I ordered a custom-made carbon recumbent in the summer of 2014.

Riding a recumbent is very different from riding on an upright bike and it took a bit of practice to get proficient. In comparison to an upright, a recumbent is heavier and therefore slower going up hills. However, it is more aerodynamic and faster going downhill and perhaps on level terrain. Overall, I felt that I was as fast on the recumbent as on an upright and I tried to fully embrace it.

Not long after I got my bike, Jacqueline noticed an advertisement for an organized recumbent ride in Ann Arbor and encouraged me to participate. It was there that I met Don Rose, a recumbent cyclist who would become my primary cycling partner. Don and I are of the same approximate age; extremely fit, he is an outstanding recumbent cyclist. Over the next several years, Don and I would do many organized centuries together, including the inaugural Baroudeur cycling event at Wayne State in 2015.

Baroudeur means fighter or warrior in French. It is also a term used in cycling for riders who are not afraid to break away from the pack and do things on their own, even if they might be an underdog. It was the perfect name for a Wayne State cycling event, as our athletic teams are known as the Warriors, and the spirit of the Baroudeur captures the Warrior Strong motto of our students.

I had initiated the Baroudeur to get people to spend time on our campus for a day of fun and exercise, to explore Detroit (the route was predominantly in the city of Detroit), and to raise scholarship funds for students. More than a thousand people registered to cycle 20, 37, 62, and 100 miles for the inaugural event. By this time, I was no longer on hormone therapy and was back to full physical and cardiovascular strength, so I opted for the 100 miles. Don and I rode together and when we got to within 20 miles of the finish, we got lost in one of Detroit's neighborhoods and added a few extra miles. We were still among the three cyclists to finish first, having cycled 102 miles in 5 hours and 12 minutes for an average speed of almost 20 mph. The other cyclist was on an upright bike.

After the success of the Baroudeur, I started another cycling event in 2017 named the Road Warrior Cycling Tour. The impetus for the event came after the 2016 presidential election. I was surprised that Donald Trump had carried Michigan because no one I routinely interacted with in the Detroit region gave him a chance of winning the state. I realized then that I needed to get out to other areas of Michigan more, particularly the rural towns, to better understand a perspective that I was not getting in Detroit. After all, Wayne State serves the entire state.

The Warrior Cycling Tour encompassed rural towns about one hundred miles apart. About seven or eight Wayne State–affiliated cyclists, and Don, traveled from town to town, beginning in Detroit and ending in Detroit five days later after cycling over five hundred miles. At each stop, we held a community reception in the evening attended by prospective students, parents, alumni, and community members and leaders to have a dialogue about higher education. We repeated the event in 2018 and 2019 along different routes. Our marketing motto was "Wayne State University—just a bike ride away."

Don and I still cycle together even though I now ride my upright again. I enjoyed my time riding the recumbent and am indebted to Don for reigniting my enthusiasm for cycling at a time when I was almost ready to give it up. At the time of this writing, my physical fitness is exceptional. It's not unusual for me to do a century ride in under five hours, and I routinely train with cycling clubs whose membership includes cyclists who race and are thirty and even forty years younger.

I am also realistic. It is sobering to know that no matter how hard I train, I will not improve physically. The best I can hope for is to slow the rate of decline, to flatten the downward curve as much as possible. I am noticing that youngsters I was coaching just a few years ago are progressively improving and now passing me. I will continue cycling for many more years; but the time has come for me to stop being so competitive. It is, after all, the natural order of things.

As a physician, I routinely encountered sight-threatening and life-threatening diseases. Experiencing them from the patient perspective was disconcerting and humbling. It is not lost on me that the course and outcome of each of my health issues was the absolute best-case scenario. To a certain extent, luck was with me. But I also recognize that I had access to the best medical care. I had terrific doctors—many of whom worked within the medical system of which I was the leader—and was treated at some of the finest facilities in the world. Most patients don't have such privilege. Some of these patients still get outstanding care; many, especially minorities and the poor, do not.

I believe that all patients should have access to the type of medical care I received. In our society, the type of care we receive and the type of outcomes we achieve are too dependent on social determinants. How is it possible that in a country as affluent as ours, a man living in southeast Washington, D.C., near where I went to high school, can have a life expectancy nineteen years shorter than that of a man living in Bethesda, Maryland, where I worked at the

NIH? The distance between where I went to high school and the NIH is nineteen miles; that's a year of life lost for every mile from NIH toward Suitland. I don't have all the answers, but health inequities such as this shine a light on an injustice that must be tackled and eradicated. The solutions are multifaceted and include fighting biases, training more minority physicians, and assuring better access to health care for all. These are causes for which I intend to devote a significant amount of time and energy after my current work as university president is completed.

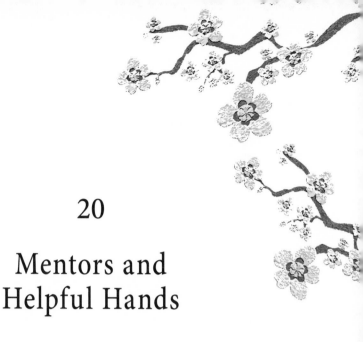

20

Mentors and Helpful Hands

I've been fortunate in my career to have had terrific mentors. One of the earliest and most influential was Brad Straatsma. I met Dr. Straatsma when I went to Los Angeles for my first real job—working in St. Lucia and going to the beach every day didn't feel like a real job. My primary position was as chief of ophthalmology at the Charles R. Drew University of Medicine and Science (CDU) and the King/Drew Medical Center (KDMC) in South Central Los Angeles. Medical students at CDU spent their first two years learning the basic and clinical sciences at the UCLA School of Medicine and the final two years doing clinical rotations at the KDMC. Because of the relationship with UCLA, I had a faculty appointment in the Jules Stein Eye Institute (JSEI) of UCLA. I spent most of my time running the ophthalmology residency program at the KDMC but spent about a day and a half per week seeing my own glaucoma patients and performing research at the JSEI.

Brad Straatsma was the founding director of the JSEI and chair of ophthalmology at UCLA. I admired him tremendously and tried to emulate his management style. He always allowed others to express their opinions before he spoke. When he did speak, he was soft-spoken, never raising his voice. His expression never changed when he was upset; the reddening of his ears was the only giveaway.

Dr. Straatsma was extraordinarily supportive of the KDMC and of me personally. Not everyone at JSEI shared his views on the KDMC and wondered why JSEI would even be bothered with the ophthalmology program there. The head of the division of glaucoma at JSEI was one such person. One day, upset with how the division chief had excluded me in a glaucoma-related media report, I stormed into Dr. Straatsma's office and complained. Instead of letting me vent my anger, he pointed out that I was deriving great benefit from my association with the JSEI and encouraged me to focus on the positives. He was correct. I had a nice personal office and two rooms to examine patients that were exclusively for my use; patient referrals were shared equally with me and the other glaucoma specialists; and I had control of my own schedule at JSEI and complete autonomy to run the program as I desired at the KDMC.

I learned a valuable lesson that day and now try to look at the positives of any given situation before getting too caught up with the negatives. But what he didn't tell me, and what I appreciated immensely, is that he did have a talk with the division chief. He must have admonished him, because the division chief was somewhat sheepish when he saw me the next day. From that day forward, his behavior toward me changed.

Dr. Straatsma made me feel that I was valued at the JSEI and that I belonged. That alone impacted my career more than anything, but his influence didn't stop there. When I discussed with him my desire to create a Center for Eye Epidemiology at the JSEI, he procured a $1 million gift from the Ahmanson Foundation to help get it started; he recommended me for accelerated promotion to professor at UCLA, and I became professor in 1994, just eight years from when I began my academic career as an assistant professor; and he introduced me to Dr. Ken Shine, who at the time was dean of the UCLA School of Medicine and later became president of the Institute of Medicine (now named National Academy of Medicine) and was another of my academic mentors.

In 1998, Dr. Straatsma nominated me for membership in the American Ophthalmological Society (AOS), the oldest specialty society in medicine, where I became the first Black member in its 138-year history in 2002. In addition to the nomination, membership in this prestigious society is dependent on acceptance of a thesis and election by the members. To be accepted as a member of AOS was a lengthy, extensive process, and it was an incredible honor. Most of my ophthalmology colleagues were glaucoma subspecialists. The AOS allowed me to develop contacts and friends from other subspecialties of ophthalmology. This proved to be important, as a touchpoint, as I became more involved with academic administration and less so with the field of ophthalmology.

I often relied on Dr. Straatsma for advice, including in 1991 when I was on a review panel for the Ocular Hypertension Treatment Study (OHTS), probably the most significant clinical trial ever conducted on the topic of glaucoma. Based on the recommendations of the review panel, the National Eye Institute (NEI) funded the study and planned to have about sixteen clinical sites. I was intimately familiar with OHTS and had applied for JSEI to be one of the clinical sites. Although the priority score the JSEI application received was high enough to have been selected, we were skipped over in favor of several sites with less favorable scores. I was extremely upset and went to Dr. Straatsma to discuss lodging a formal complaint with the NEI. He advised me against it. "Roy," he said in his typical quiet voice, "I think that you have a bright future and the potential to be selected to be on the NEI Advisory Council in the future. Don't blow it." I had been on many NEI review panels; but the Advisory Council was the highest-level advisory body for the NEI, and members wielded substantial influence on ophthalmic research priorities. Although he understood why I was so upset, he did not want me to risk this possible honor by getting into an antagonistic relationship with the NEI and its leadership.

I consequently decided to approach the situation differently. I did not protest. Many years later, in 2016, I was invited to join the NEI Advisory Council, just as he had predicted, as well as the NIH Advisory Council to the Director, the highest-level advisory body for the entire NIH. I had acted out of emotion whereas Dr. Straatsma had a longer-range view. I'm glad I learned this lesson early in my career.

Incidentally, the JSEI did become a clinical site, but not through the usual channels. The person who was instrumental in making that happen was John Ruffin, the director of the Office of Research on Minority Health (ORMH) of the NIH. This office was created by Dr. Louis Sullivan in 1990 when he was U.S. secretary of health and human services. It evolved into the Center for Minority Health and Health Disparities and then in 2010, with congressional legislation, became the National Institute on Minority Health and Health Disparities (NIMHD). These changes seem small but were important in raising the profile of minority research, in providing grant funding authorization, and in garnering more resources.

John's influence increased as the ORMH evolved into the NIMHD, and he used it to level the playing field for many Black researchers. During the review phase of the OHTS, Michael Drake, a colleague and friend who was also on the review panel, and I had both argued that since glaucoma disproportionately affected Blacks, the sampling strategy should include more Black subjects. As director of ORMH John agreed, and also felt that more Black investigators needed to be part of the study. He agreed to fund an additional six sites with the condition that both Michael Drake and I were included as principal investigators for our respective sites.

Scores of other Black investigators benefited over the years because John made sure that they were treated fairly. Most of them did not know that he intervened on their behalf. He didn't publicize it; he just did it because he could and that's the kind of extra assistance that many white investigators routinely received.

Michael Drake is another person who greatly influenced me, in this case to go into glaucoma as my career specialty. We met in Boston when Michael was a glaucoma fellow at the MEEI and I was an ophthalmology resident. Our careers have mirrored each other's, and as colleagues, we have provided friendship and counsel to each other over the years. We also share several passionate interests, including cycling and wine.

Michael is a few years older than me and was on the glaucoma faculty at the University of California, San Francisco, when I was finishing my ophthalmology residency. I went to visit him as I was trying to decide whether to go into glaucoma or another specialty and I needed career guidance. I will never forget his graciousness at that meeting.

There are not a lot of Blacks in ophthalmology and most are in clinical practice. When limited to academic faculty, in 2019, a little more than 2 percent of ophthalmology faculty were Black. That proportion would have been even lower decades earlier when we had our meeting. When further limited to academic faculty specializing in glaucoma—well, there are very few. Those of us who have made it to that level are accustomed to being the "only one" in the group, and there is a certain lure to being recognized in that way. It would not have surprised me if Michael had steered me in another direction, or at least had been unenthusiastic about me pursuing glaucoma as my specialty. After all, I could have been viewed as future competition.

He took me to a private tennis club and we had a glass of wine. When I explained my career indecision, he quickly got to the point and insisted that I pursue glaucoma. He loved the specialty and believed that I would also. Rather than viewing me as potential competition, he welcomed me into the specialty. "It would be great if we were colleagues," he said. I decided to pursue glaucoma on the spot.

Over the years, our careers have tracked remarkably similarly, from rising through the academic ranks as glaucoma faculty, to holding significant medical school leadership positions, to becoming university chancellors/presidents at several universities. Through this time, we've supported and encouraged each other. Many positions we hold and honors we've received have been through the recommendation and advocacy of the other. I learned through our relationship that so much more can be achieved through collaboration and by helping each other—even if that means sharing the limelight—than by competing and being the "only one." As an example, Michael was elected to the National Academy of Medicine several years before I was. I later learned that he was one of the two sponsors who recommended me for membership.

No matter how talented one may believe one is, the truth is that we all receive assistance from others, even if that assistance is not publicly displayed. Such has been the order of business for centuries for those privileged enough to attend elite prep schools and universities, join exclusive clubs, and have influential parents. For most of the history of the United States, such privilege did not extend to minorities and the financially disadvantaged.

I am under no illusion that my accomplishments have been unassisted. That is in part why I try to help others in their career goals. I've been particularly drawn to assisting students who have dealt with difficult life circumstances but are attempting to overcome them and persevere, and even thrive.

For an Alumni Profile for the 2002 edition of *Allegheny* magazine, I was asked which of my accolades and accomplishments I was most proud of. I answered that none of my accomplishments meant as much to me as giving underrepresented and underprivileged students the opportunity to become excellent physicians and ophthalmologists. It was still relatively early in my career, but I had been responsible for selecting many ophthalmology residency candidates, most of whom did not have a chance of getting accepted into other programs, into my program at Charles Drew University. I saw something special in them and took a chance. In almost every case, my faith in them was validated. I further elaborated that "my proudest accomplishment was being able to see these individuals having an impact throughout the country and knowing that I had some influence in their careers."

I hesitate to name any of these resident trainees because I am proud of all of them. However, I will mention a few illustrative examples.

Tim Goodwin was the first resident I selected. He was an emergency room physician who wanted to change his specialty and become an ophthalmologist. We were about the same age, but he always showed deference and treated me with utmost respect. In the same way that I had difficulty calling Dr. Straatsma "Brad," he wouldn't call me "Roy" until recently. Tim performed a glaucoma fellowship at UCLA after his residency and set up a practice in Inglewood, a predominantly Black community in Los Angeles.

I trusted Tim enough that I confided in him about my glaucoma diagnosis after he had established his practice. He occasionally performed visual field tests for me and provided me with medication as needed so that I didn't have to have a prescription filled by a pharmacy. Tim is one of the only Black glaucoma fellowship–trained ophthalmologists in the Los Angeles area, and he has been serving a great need in the community for decades.

Maurice Syrquin was another ophthalmology candidate whom I selected even though he did not have the stellar credentials other programs were requiring. He had not matched in ophthalmology and was performing a surgical internship at Beth Israel Hospital in Boston when I received a note from the legendary Bill Silen, the chair of surgery at Beth Israel, recommending Maurice in laudatory terms. I knew from Dr. Silen's reputation as well as from personal experience that he was not easily impressed. I had performed my medical school surgery rotation with him and seen firsthand how he outworked everyone including the interns and residents, beginning each day with patient rounds at 4:30 a.m.

With such a compelling recommendation, there was no way I could not take a chance on Maurice. After his residency, he performed both medical and surgical vitreoretinal fellowships at UCLA and then set up a very successful practice with the Retina Institute of Texas in Dallas.

I met Steve Jack in New York through my friend Nancy. Steve graduated from Cornell's medical school but did not match. He was not a good test-taker and didn't get high enough board scores to match into the highly competitive field of ophthalmology. But I knew him to be a kind and compassionate person who loved medicine. He had traveled far in life to get to his level of achievement and that counted for something. Besides, he was a friend of Nancy's and she believed in him. After he successfully completed his residency, he went to Guam to practice ophthalmology and has been there ever since.

Another career I helped advance was that of Rick Baker. Rick and I became friends in medical school through Barry. We were close enough that he was best man at my first wedding. Rick was raised by his grandmother in Harlem and overcame many obstacles. He was extremely gifted academically, but he had one major limitation. "Procrastination" doesn't quite capture it, but that was part of the problem. Rick would just get "stuck" and not progress to completing things on an expected timeline. He would ultimately always complete whatever it was that he was working on, but it would be on his timeline.

I met Rick while he was a student in the Harvard-MIT Health Sciences and Technology (HST) program, which was a unique collaboration between HMS and MIT to integrate science, medicine, and engineering to solve problems in human health. HMS was selective enough; the Harvard-MIT HST program was ultra-selective. I always thought that Rick was the smartest of the group of us who were friends in medical school.

Rick was interested in epidemiology, so I introduced him to Alec Walker, the epidemiologist at the Harvard School of Public Health with whom I performed my first research study on glaucoma risk factors, and they did a project together. Alec would call me periodically to ask about Rick because he hadn't heard from him. I always assured him that Rick would come through with whatever it was that he was supposed to do in due course. One day, he just showed up and handed Alec his completed work. Alec was surprised but he also thought that the work product was outstanding. That's just how Rick functioned.

Rick graduated a few years later and then went to the University of Minnesota to perform a medical internship, followed by further studies in epidemiology. Some of Rick's research work was on diabetic retinopathy and he became interested in pursuing an ophthalmology residency. Rick applied to my program but his candidacy presented a bit of a conundrum. He was obviously intelligent and had many more publications than the average applicant. On the other hand, he had bounced around a bit and didn't seem to have a clear career direction. I knew Rick would be fine and supported him. But I didn't want to be the sole decision maker since we were friends. I presented Rick's candidacy to the ophthalmology faculty, and Rick was interviewed. As expected, everyone was impressed and he was taken outside the match. Rick has had a very successful career in medical administration at Charles R. Drew University of Medicine and Science and at Wayne State University.

I had more limited opportunities to be helpful to specific individuals once I became the dean of the medical school. However, one individual immediately comes to mind. Susan was a struggling young medical student who was living a difficult life. She was a Latina single mother who was interested in pursuing emergency medicine in the south-central Los Angeles neighborhood where she was born and raised. I knew her because of her volunteer work in the community and was impressed with her commitment. It had come to my attention that Susan was encountering financial difficulty that was jeopardizing her continued enrollment in school. I obtained her bank account information and anonymously deposited five hundred dollars per month for most of her senior year. Years later, the university's vice president for finance alerted me that a former medical student who was now an emergency room doctor was attempting to pay back funds provided to her as a student but that there was no record of these transactions. I confided in the vice president and let her know that I had assisted the student with my personal funds; I asked her to let this former student know that the "university" had forgiven the debt.

I went out of my way to help Susan anonymously because someone had helped me in that way during my senior year of medical school. After my rotations at Oxford, I was beyond broke. I had to pay for housing at Oxford as well as keep up the rental payments in Boston to ensure I had somewhere to live when I returned. I had also encountered trouble with my car, Big Yellow. Before I left for Oxford, I had loaned Big Yellow to a friend. It was "booted" while parked and rather than pay the parking tickets to have the boot taken off, he abandoned it. Eventually, it was towed. When I returned to Boston and went to retrieve my car, it was gone. The towing company said it had been junked but I knew it had been sold. I had just spent a considerable amount of money to restore it, putting in a new interior and giving it a fresh coat of paint.

I was within months of graduating but was behind on rent, had no car, and had maxed out my credit cards. I was in substantial debt with no means to get out of it. What saved me was two thousand dollars that someone anonymously put into my bank account. To this day, I have no idea who it was. But I told myself that when a situation arose wherein I could do the same to help a medical student in similar circumstances, I would. Susan gave me the opportunity to fulfill that pledge.

Being a mentor has many rewards, among which is the deep satisfaction experienced when a mentee surpasses your expectations. Such was the case with Fotis Topouzis. In 1996, the Scientific Advisory Board of the Glaucoma Research Foundation, of which I was a member, decided to support international candidates from less developed countries for a fellowship year with mentors from the United States. Fotis had applied for consideration and I selected him over many other candidates to work with me and my colleague Anne Coleman at the Jules Stein Eye Institute.

Fotis is Greek and he performed his ophthalmology training in Paris. English was his third language and he was barely adequate at it. But he worked hard and his English, both oral and written, improved considerably during his fellowship. Like me, Anne had also gone to the UCLA School of Public Health to receive training in epidemiology. Fotis became interested in epidemiology that year, and with our assistance, he designed and planned a glaucoma prevalence study to be performed in his home country. That study, the Thessaloniki Eye Study, became one of the most important glaucoma epidemiological studies worldwide.

Anne and I helped Fotis navigate the politics of academia in Greece, and he is currently chair of the Department of Ophthalmology at Aristotle University and president of the European Glaucoma Society. It would be difficult to identify a more prominent European glaucoma specialist than Fotis. I am extremely proud of his accomplishments.

I'm sure I exceeded Dr. Straatsma's expectations of me because, in truth, they were initially low. Early in my career, he was providing counsel in his role as department chair and warned me that I might have difficulties getting promoted from assistant professor to associate professor because of my field of scholarship. Although he didn't come out and say it, I got the impression that he did not believe epidemiology to be real science. In contrast, he highlighted the basic science laboratory work of another assistant professor as the prototypical type of research that would be viewed favorably by promotion and tenure committees.

At UCLA, as at many academic institutions, faculty had seven years to get promoted to associate professor and get tenure. Those who were unsuccessful were required to seek employment elsewhere. The assistant professor mentioned by Dr. Straatsma was not successful and he left academic ophthalmology for private practice. I was promoted from assistant professor to associate professor in four years and received accelerated promotion to full professor in eight. To date, I am the only Black person to have achieved the rank of full professor at the Jules Stein Eye Institute.

In a good mentor-mentee relationship, as occurred with Ms. Stephan, both parties grow and gain new perspectives. In 2020, Anne Coleman—a JSEI faculty member, prominent glaucoma epidemiologist, and mentee of Dr. Straatsma's—was the president of the American Academy of Ophthalmology, and Dr. Straatsma and I were both her honored guests at the annual meeting. It would be safe to speculate that Dr. Straatsma's perspectives on epidemiology have changed.

21

Dad II

I vowed not to be like my dad and spent a good part of my life living up to that pledge. At social events, I'm usually one of the first to leave, never the last (unless I'm hosting). Once I completed my medical training, I never rented a place to live but always bought something, even when doing so might not have been the best financial decision. I drink alcohol, almost exclusively wine with an occasional martini, but never get drunk. I try to be positive and encourage my children, not negative and overly critical. When they were younger, I took my family on annual vacations, usually to destinations around the world, and never spared expenses.

These behaviors were a reaction to the father I knew growing up. My children, Yoshio and Presley, however, remember their grandfather quite differently, as a kindhearted, caring man who loved to spend time with them. Krista, Dianna's daughter, also describes him in similar adoring terms.

But people have the ability to change. My dad stopped drinking alcohol in 1992 after my son, Yoshio, was born. I told Dad that Yoshio would not be allowed in any vehicle he was driving. At the time, he did not believe he was an alcoholic and had a discussion with Dianna, who admonished him in stark terms. "This is going to affect your relationship with your grandson. What are you going to do about it, Dad?" she asked. "Hold on tightly to the belief that you couldn't be an alcoholic, or educate yourself about what problem drinking is?" Despite being skeptical, he started regularly attending rehabilitation classes at the military hospital and learned that he was indeed an alcoholic. Once he understood this basic fact, he never took another drink to the day he died, not even a sip.

Dad also became much more generous with his money. After Mom died and his dreams of retiring and traveling with her were lost, he spent almost nothing on himself but was very giving toward others. I learned after his death that he loaned his nephew, Floyd, a large sum of money to help him out with his car repair business. He also loaned Dianna and Brian the down payment for their house and paid to carpet their home. Whenever we went out to eat, he wanted to pay. For the first time in his life, he even had a credit card.

My dad was a practical man. He was not frivolous and he certainly was not showy. At my college graduation, when Marina's dad had presented her with a brand-new Camaro with a ribbon and bow parked conspicuously on the street next to our dormitory, Dad gave me a car as well. It was a used 1966 Plymouth Fury that Floyd had fixed up for him. But my dad gave it to me without fanfare when we got back home. I cherished that car—Big Yellow—and it held up through medical school and my ophthalmology residency years.

They say a cat has nine lives, but I'm sure Big Yellow had more. It was stolen countless times and always retrieved. It was an old car and probably not worth keeping but it was easy to steal. Usually it was stolen for a joyride and recovered the next day. It was even recovered after it was booted and towed during my Oxford trip. One of my friends saw it being driven one day, weeks after I thought it was lost for good, and reported it to the police. I got my car back and the towing company had to reimburse the person who bought it. I kept that car until I had to leave for St. Lucia in 1985.

Dad never did buy a home, or even rent a permanent home. Rather, he spent much of his time in a weekly rental facility in downtown San Diego. It was old and run-down but clean. A few homeless sheltered on the sidewalk leading up to the door, but the neighborhood was safe enough and very walkable.

He had settled on San Diego because it was warm, and he had access to good health care at the naval hospital. My dad would pay with cash for months at a time in advance for his temporary lodging. He was such a desirable customer that the management always kept a room available for him.

If my dad wasn't in San Diego, he was with me and my family wherever we were living or with my sister in Shoreline, Washington. When he was with us, Yoshio and Presley enjoyed being with him. When he was in Shoreline, he stayed with Dianna and her husband, Bob, but spent a lot of time with Krista and her family. Although Dad was frustrated with Dianna's gambling, he loved her deeply and worried a lot about her. And whatever issues Dianna may have had with Dad earlier in her life, her attitude toward him changed. Maturation on her part was likely part of the reason for this change; Dad's evolution into a different person was likely also responsible. At the time, I didn't know if Dad suspected that Dianna was not his biological child. If he did, it didn't seem to matter—Dianna was his baby girl.

I visited him after he had undergone a major surgical procedure at the naval hospital. He had intermittent claudication of his calf from years of smoking and needed vascular surgery. His postoperative recovery was rough. Fortunately, he survived; but for a while there was some uncertainty, and I gained access to his room at his living facility to collect his belongings.

The room was small, about half the size of a typical hotel room. The only furniture was a twin bed and lampstand with a small portable CD player. Dad enjoyed watching television so there was probably a small one in the room, although I don't remember seeing it. There was not enough space to fit a desk and chair. I opened his closet and was stunned to see hardly any clothes: a few pairs of slacks, a few shirts, and one pair of shoes. My dad had worked his entire life and was now retired and in his late sixties. Yet, all of his possessions could be placed inside a single suitcase, a small one at that.

Dad had his routine, which included watching sports on television, particularly football. Once he took an extended trip to Australia. He was not very open about it, but the trip seemed to involve a woman he had met who lived in Australia. It had been a couple of decades since my mom had died, so I'm not sure why he was being so secretive; but he didn't leave a forwarding address. I believe he had intended to live in Australia with this woman, but it didn't work out and he returned after about six months. The only explanation he ever offered about his return was that it was strange living there, particularly since there was no football.

I later learned from Dianna, who had found some hidden letters, that he was tight-lipped about the experience because he'd been embarrassed and hurt. The woman he went to live with was a mail-order scammer who took Dad for a significant amount of money. He'd been a good target because he was lonely and open to travel; he'd already lived in many foreign countries. Dianna's explanation made a lot more sense than Dad's account of Australia being strange and his missing football. When she told me this story, I felt sad for him.

Before he passed away, Dad had a live-in arrangement with Kinobu, the mother of my second wife, Suzanne. Kinobu lived in Tulsa, Oklahoma. She was elderly and living by herself, and Dad was elderly and without a permanent place of residence. They were able to support each other and share expenses. It was a good arrangement.

One day after returning to Tulsa from visiting Dianna, he experienced shortness of breath. After a few days of not feeling completely well, he went to see a physician who diagnosed a pulmonary embolism and admitted him to the hospital. A pulmonary embolism is a blockage of the pulmonary arteries in the lung caused by a blood clot that travels from the deep veins of the legs. This is not uncommon in elderly people, who tend to sit for long periods of time without physical activity as on an airplane. When treated, the death rate is low, around 8 percent.

He was symptomatic but not in distress and his hospitalization should have been routine. For some reason, his condition deteriorated and he was transferred to the intensive care unit, as he had developed pneumonia and had some difficulty breathing. After apparently stabilizing—I didn't see him during this time so cannot verify that to have been the case—he went to a step-down unit for monitoring. I decided to go to Tulsa to check up on him.

As soon as I stepped off the elevator at his care facility, I heard a loud moaning from one of the rooms. For a fleeting moment, it reminded me of how Dad had sounded when he was unconscious and recovering from his vascular surgery in San Diego. Since he was supposedly stable, I reasoned that the moaning could not be coming from him. But as I walked down the long hallway in the direction of his room, there was no mistaking it: the moaning was coming from Dad's room.

I entered his room and found him incoherent and in distress. No one was looking after him. I rushed to the nursing station and found the nurses there seemingly oblivious to his condition. Their nonchalance suggested that Dad's distress was not acute. He had likely been suffering for quite some time, and they had tuned him out. Incensed, I demanded to see the attending doctor. When he came out to see me, I confronted him with detailed questions about my dad's care. I wanted to make sure that the attending doctor and the nurses knew that someone was going to be monitoring his care.

Over the next few days, he was diagnosed with a hospital-acquired infection in his blood. He likely already had this infection when I first saw him. His prognosis was not good, and I informed Dianna and his grandkids, Yoshio, Presley, and Krista, in case they wanted to see him. Suzanne was already in Tulsa. The others flew in. He never regained consciousness and passed away on October 10, 2008. I wish I had been able to say a proper goodbye before he died.

To this day, I believe that Dad should not have died. Until I entered the picture and made demands upon the doctors and nurses, he was just another inconsequential Black man, being ignored despite his obvious distress. I remember him groaning and grappling to pull the nasopharyngeal tube out of his nose. I regret that he had to be in such discomfort while dying—it will haunt me forever. Had I arrived earlier, I could have made sure he was receiving adequate and appropriate care.

We buried my dad at the Parklawn Memorial Park and Menorah Gardens in Rockville, Maryland, next to my mother. I had learned of it when Marina's mother had died. It's a beautiful place—more like a park than a cemetery. I knew I wanted my parents to be buried there when their time came and had bought plots for them in advance. They didn't indulge in anything nice when they were alive; I wanted to make sure they had the nicest cemetery and nicest plots for their final resting place.

The funeral was attended by all of my dad's family from Youngstown and those living in Maryland. Yoshio later commented about how everyone there spoke so affectionately of him. Dad definitely had a different side to him than the one that informed my earliest memories. He was beloved by many. I'm glad that Yoshio and Presley got to know him in the latter stages of his life when he was a different person than the one I knew as a child.

Dad never displayed much emotion. The only time I ever saw him cry was when his father died. I likewise cried when Dad died.

I will not understate the emotional harm he caused during my childhood. I never understood why, but he was incapable of physical affection. But he did show me affection, in the only ways he knew how. He was showing me affection by waiting until I came home from school to catch pitches from me, by attending all my sports events and vociferously urging me on, by gifting me with Big Yellow. I remember Dad's words when his father died: "He wasn't perfect, but he was a good man." My dad had his shortcomings, but he was a good man. I no longer doubt that he loved me.

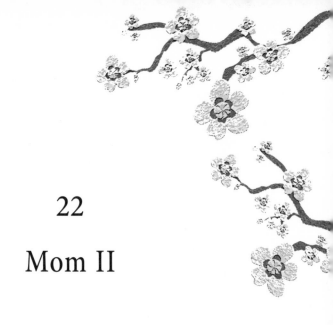

22

Mom II

My mom never really acclimated to living in the United States. She missed Japan. She missed the food, she missed the language, she missed her friends, she missed gambling. Although she managed conversational English, she never learned to read it. When we moved to Suitland in 1968, there was only one Japanese restaurant in Washington, D.C., Sakura, and it was on the opposite side of town. There weren't many Asians of any nationality in the area, let alone any who were Japanese. In fact, according to the 1970 census, only .09 percent of the population of Maryland were Japanese.

Mom had only one friend in the United States, a Japanese woman, Umi, who lived not far from us. Umi had also married a Black serviceman. She was a seamstress and performed alterations at the local dry cleaners. Incredibly, Umi knew my mother from Japan during the time that I was running away from home. She even occasionally saw me at the train station in Sayama, traveling alone to another town. Umi often spoke of seeing me and being puzzled as to why I was alone. What a small world!

Why, then, did my mom leave Japan? It was probably not for love, although she and my dad did ultimately have a very supportive relationship. She even got into football and often watched the Washington Redskins on television with Dad. Mom likely realized that the only way she would stop gambling was if she left that environment in Japan. But I doubt that was the primary reason she left everything she loved. I asked myself that question a lot—Why did Mom leave Japan?—though I suspect I knew the answer. I'm now sure of it: she did it for me.

My understanding of the samurai is now much more nuanced than it was as a child. Arguably the greatest swordsmen in history, many were brutal and ruthless, even when not engaged in combat, and many used their nobility and higher status to subjugate and bully the peasant class of farmers and workers. I idealized the samurais from what I saw of them in the movies, but my perception was overly simplistic.

I had likewise idealized Japan and many aspects of its culture. But as I matured, I began to see things in a different light. Like the samurai, the Japanese also tend to be insular and arrogant. The country has a history of racism and xenophobia that still permeates society. More than 97 percent of Japan's population are ethnically Japanese; the remainder are foreign nationals residing in Japan. Access to education and jobs is limited for those who are not ethnically Japanese. My mother understood what I have now come to understand: I never would have been accepted in Japan. I would have been subjected to racism and discrimination that would have impacted my ability to succeed in that society.

It would not have mattered that I was born in Japan to a Japanese mother. My mother was acutely aware of this fact because of her own experiences. She often told me stories about how the Japanese reacted when Americans, particularly Black Americans, first came to Japan after World War II. Many expected Blacks to have tails, like monkeys, and were surprised when they didn't. She was treated as an outcast when she married my father; more hurtful, she was shunned by friends.

Mom was also painfully aware that the Japanese value very white skin, especially for women. Japanese women are very careful to protect their face and body from the sun. She rarely spoke about her family; when she did, it was almost always about her sister. Because she had scoliosis, her sister likely did not work outdoors. Mom often reminisced about how people thought her sister was so white and beautiful. Mom had relatively darker skin from years of working outdoors in the rice fields. She once commented that she wished she had been the one to suffer an early death instead of her sister. Mom loved her sister, but I think she also envied her white skin.

One of the unwritten codes of the samurai was self-sacrifice in the pursuit of a higher goal. Leaving Japan to live in the United States was my mom's self-sacrifice; her higher goal was for her son to have an opportunity to succeed.

Although I've had to overcome bias and racism, the opportunities I've been afforded in the United States have undoubtedly been much greater than they would have been in Japan. A driving factor in my life has been to make sure that my mom's sacrifice was not in vain.

Mom led a fairly quiet life in Maryland. She stayed in the same Shady Grove apartments in Suitland where we lived when I was in high school for quite a while. Umi was her only friend and she spent a lot of time with Kimi, her Chinese pug. Then she and Dad moved to another apartment complex further into the suburbs of Prince George County, near the Capital Centre, where the Washington Bullets of the NBA played. The apartment was a little nicer, but it was also more isolated. Mom would love it when I came home to visit and she would cook my favorite dish, shrimp tempura.

To assist with family finances, she took a job in housekeeping at a local Holiday Inn. She kept that job from the time I was in high school until she moved to the apartment near the Capital Centre. Because she didn't drive, either Dad or I would drop her off and pick her up as necessary. I recall how happy she was when someone left a generous tip. She appreciated a tip of even a few dollars; but occasionally someone would leave her a twenty, and she would be absolutely ecstatic. I consequently always tip well when I stay at hotels.

My mom was never pretentious and didn't like people who were. She thought that Marina and her family were pretentious, and she was hopeful that we would not get married. She did want grandchildren, though, and she wanted me to get married to someone and have kids before she died. Unfortunately, she passed away well before either Yoshio or Presley was born, when she was only fifty-four years old.

I'm uncertain why, but Mom often commented that she was going to die young. "Roy-san, I'm going to die soon so please listen to me," she would implore as she attempted to give me advice on this or that issue. She was healthy and did not take any medications. Except for smoking, she had nothing in her medical history that was of concern. Her diet consisted primarily of rice, fish, and vegetables. She rarely ate anything fried or fatty. I actually don't remember her ever seeking medical care, not even for a routine physical. There was no rational reason for my mom to make such a statement and I basically ignored it.

Once Mom became ill, her condition progressed rapidly. It started off with a cough and some difficulty breathing. When Dad mentioned that she was beginning to cough up blood, I knew the situation was likely serious and insisted that she seek medical attention. Mom initially refused but finally agreed, and she was evaluated by one of the military doctors at Andrews Air Force Base.

I was beginning my third year as an ophthalmology resident at the MEEI at the time. For some reason, unrelated to her illness, I was home for a few days, so I accompanied her on a follow-up visit. Knowing that I was a physician, the treating doctor showed me her chest X-ray. There was a mass in one of the lungs, and I knew it was likely a tumor. Subsequent biopsy confirmed what I feared: it was a small cell carcinoma, the most aggressive form of lung cancer.

Mom was a very stoic woman. She rarely expressed any sort of emotion. As close as we were, she never displayed any physical affection, not even an occasional hug. True to form, when Mom was told of her diagnosis and the prognosis, she didn't express any fear or even show signs of apprehension.

I wanted to stay home for a few days to be with my mom. However, she insisted I go back to Boston and I reluctantly did so. She progressively deteriorated and, after about six months, she was hospitalized on and off to undergo various tests, procedures, and treatments. It was now the beginning of December and I was looking forward to going home for the holiday in a few weeks. One early afternoon, when I was seeing patients in the clinic, Dad called to let me know Mom was not doing well. I continued to see patients but was obviously distracted. John Woog, one of my third-year co-residents, knew that my mother was battling cancer and told me to fly home immediately. He took over my patients and basically kicked me out of the clinic.

I will forever be grateful to John. My sense of duty was such that I was torn between fulfilling my responsibilities to my patients and seeing my mom. If I had completed my clinic, I would not have been able to get a flight until the following day. Because of John, I was able to leave Boston that same afternoon.

When I got home, Mom was cheerful and we had an intimate conversation. The following morning, she became disoriented and her speech was slurred. I recognized her symptoms—particularly when I smelled a distinctive sweetness in her breath—as that of hepatic encephalopathy, a nervous system disorder brought on by severe liver disease. My mom had developed cirrhosis, a liver disease most commonly caused by hepatitis and alcohol abuse. Since she didn't have hepatitis and never drank alcohol, the cause of the liver failure was a mystery. By process of elimination, it was attributed to possible past trauma; although Mom never blamed Dad, she confided in me that she thought it could have been from the stomach kick she received from him during their fight after her first time gambling. Whatever the cause, a liver with cirrhosis doesn't work properly and the toxins that build up in the blood travel to the brain and cause a decline in its function.

Over the next several days, Mom floated in and out of consciousness. Because I had taken care of a lot of patients with hepatic encephalopathy at Harlem Hospital Center, I knew the end was near. Knowing that she would not want extraordinary measures taken to keep her alive, I requested that she be discharged from the hospital and released to home care.

My dad and I took turns taking care of her in her final days. On the evening of December 17, 1983, she asked Dad to help her bathe. As a Japanese woman, Mom loved her baths. Afterward, he dressed her in a nice kimono and went back to the living room to watch football on television. I sat next to her as she lay in her bed and patiently waited for periods of lucidity and coherence so that we could converse. There was so much more about her side of the family I wanted to know about—my grandfather, grandmother, uncle, and aunt. But these periods when we could communicate were short, and I let her talk about whatever was on her mind.

I still remember the peaceful look in her eyes in her final moments of lucidity. Mom took my hand in hers, gazed directly into my eyes, and whispered her last words: "Roy-san, everyone makes mistakes. You must learn to forgive. Roy-san, you must forgive." And then she closed her eyes and was gone.

I sat there, holding her hands and contemplating her last words for a long while before going out to tell my dad she had died. What was Mom trying to tell me? What must I forgive? Whom must I forgive? Was she referring to herself? Dianna? Perhaps Dad? I had reason to feel anger and resentment toward all three, as well as others, and I was not sure whom—or what—she wanted me to forgive.

Eventually I went to the living room. "Dad, she died," I said. Initially, he didn't comprehend what I was trying to tell him. He must have thought I was just making a general comment about Mom not doing well because his reply was a puzzling, "I know." I grabbed hold of both his shoulders, firmly shook him, and repeated, "No, Dad, you're not listening. Mom is dead." After finally comprehending, he was inconsolable. Dad babbled on about how he had just bathed her, about the wonderful conversation they had just had together, about how she thanked him for taking care of her, about how peaceful and content she seemed.

It was then that I realized how much they had come to mean to each other. Whatever difficulties they may have had in their earlier relationship, they had become settled in each other's lives and needed each other. Both had evolved into different people individually and they had evolved as a couple. I don't know if I would go so far as to claim that there was a deep love between them. But, as Mom whispered, "Everyone makes mistakes," and I think they had come to accept each other and had forgiven each other for their imperfections and transgressions.

For years, even decades, I've wondered about whom and what Mom wanted me to forgive. She understood me better than anyone. She knew that I had harbored a simmering rage throughout most of my life and that some of it still lingered below the surface. She knew that this rage needed release, like a volcano that lies dormant for ages and suddenly erupts. She worried about that.

As a child, I stuttered uncontrollably. As I got older, I compensated by beating everyone up. The slightest provocation, whether on the road or basketball courts, would set me off. Even channeling my underlying insecurities to excel in everything I did—though more productive and socially acceptable—was not healthy. I certainly had reasons to be angry with others in my life. But there was something else she understood.

As I've matured, I've learned that relationships can be complicated. No one else, besides the two involved, can really understand the intricate dynamics of what keeps two people together, or what breaks them apart. The relationship between Mom and Dad was complicated, but in the end, they both seemed content. They derived nourishment and support from each other, and it was a wonderful thing to witness.

I'm now convinced that Dad knew that Dianna was not his biological daughter. I never discussed it with him, so I will never know for sure; but one look at Dianna would convince any unbiased person that she was fully Asian. I believe now that he knew but didn't care, that he and Mom had worked through this issue in their relationship and that both had moved on from it. In fact, it's possible that he knew before he and Mom got married in 1958, just a couple of months before Dianna was born. I've come to understand also that for Dianna, it never was an issue. She never felt less than his daughter, even in the toughest of times. I asked her recently whether she thought Dad knew that she was not his biological daughter. She replied, "That sounds very odd to me. I was his only daughter, his baby girl, and he was my dad. And that was that."

The only person who had not moved on was me. Since that day fifty years ago, when I was told by Brian that Dad was not Dianna's father, the subject never came up. A switch turned off for me that never turned back on. My relationship with Dianna changed and I disengaged. Throughout the years, I've pondered the reasons behind my reaction. Part of it was because of her gambling addiction. But I'm very understanding of human frailties and try not to judge people harshly because of them. Deep down, I know that I never let it go.

Until then, Dianna and I had a bond forged out of the common experience of growing up without parental presence and oversight, honing survival skills and depending on each other. I felt a responsibility to take care of her and never resented having to do so. I was her big brother. Perhaps I reacted the way I did because I felt that I should have done more to help her. Perhaps I felt that I had failed my little sister.

Many decades later, I've come to realize that the specifics of whom or what my mother had in mind doesn't matter. I think she knew that I needed to resolve the anger and resentment I had been harboring in order to enjoy life to the fullest. I needed to forgive her. I needed to forgive Dad. I needed to forgive Dianna. Most importantly, I needed to forgive myself. "Roy-san, everyone makes mistakes . . . you must forgive."

What happened next was profoundly meaningful and symbolic. Before a funeral home can proceed with arrangements for someone who has died, there must be an official declaration of death. Dad had been instructed to call the hospital when Mom died; they would send an ambulance to get her and bring her to the emergency room to have a doctor sign an official death certificate.

As he was about to make the call, it occurred to me that I was now a doctor. In the emergency room of Harlem Hospital Center, I had declared many patients dead and had signed many death certificates. I had the authority to do so.

The most difficult thing I ever did in my life, and yet at the same time the most rewarding, was to be able, as a doctor, to pronounce my mom dead and sign her death certificate. She was thereby spared the indignity of having to go to an emergency room. My final image of Mom as she was transported directly to the funeral home was that of a dignified woman with a look of peace on her face.

Mom had brought me into this world; I officially declared her as no longer of this world. Because of the sacrifices she had made throughout her life, I was able to become a doctor and ensure that she was treated with dignity and respect when she died. That would have been important to her.

There comes a point during medical training when you realize what it means to be a doctor, when you understand the awesome responsibility you've accepted and taken an oath to fulfill. For me, this was that time.

Mom was buried at Parklawn Memorial Park and Menorah Gardens, where Dad would also eventually be buried. I had bought a plot on a hill facing the direction of Japan. As I said my final goodbyes to Mom, I carefully laid the plum tree etching she had purchased for me as a child inside the coffin next to her. On it was written the following inscription in Japanese: "The plum tree blossoms even in winter." Typically appearing in February, the month of Mom's birth, plum blossoms come to life even while covered in frost. Unfazed by the cold, they endure, overcoming the adversity of winter.

The day Mom bought me that etching was one of my earliest memories of being with her. I was deeply drawn to it. Somewhat metaphysical in my world-view as a child, I often sought deeper meaning in simple expressions. The plum blossom is imbued with symbolism. For me, it symbolized my hopes for Mom to return home after yet another disappointing Christmas alone as a child.

It symbolized something else, too. My mom's death was a dark time, and I drew strength from the plum blossom as I did countless times growing up. The plum blossom symbolized beauty—beauty that emerges even in the bleakest of times.

The enormity of Mom's death came down on me the night before the funeral. Up to that point, I was busy making funeral and other arrangements. My boys from medical school and New York came to be with me. Barry came late that night when most of the guests had left, took me into the bathroom, and sat me down. "How you feeling?" was all he asked and neither of us uttered another word. Sitting there in silence, I reflected on my time with Mom, just the two of us, in Yokohama; on her cooking me shrimp tempura whenever I came home for a visit, no matter how late it was; on how proud she was of me. Then, tears welled up and I cried uncontrollably.

The next day, as Mom's casket was lowered into the ground and realizing that she would no longer be a part of my life, I felt an emptiness that needed to be filled. Knowing that the Japanese plum tree was with her provided me assurance that tomorrow would come and be a brighter day. As a final token of acknowledging her homeland, I had a rising sun, the motif for the Japanese flag, carved on her bronze headstone.

In the years that followed, I wanted to do more to honor my mom. During one of our conversations during her illness, I learned that she had wanted to give me a Japanese name—Masao. She told me that in Kanji—Japanese writing using Chinese characters—Masao meant "righteous" or "true man." My dad wasn't having it and named me "Roy." But I never had a middle name. Growing up, I was conscious of the fact that everyone else seemed to have a middle name or initial.

I decided I would add "Masao" to my formal name, that it would be my first name. However, since I was an adult and everyone knew me as Roy, I decided to use the initial "M" and to still go by "Roy." I use "M. Roy Wilson" on all my formal, and "mrw" on all my informal, communications. Officially though, as of November 21, 1986, my first name is Masao. In this way, I continue to honor the woman who sacrificed so much for her son.

Epilogue

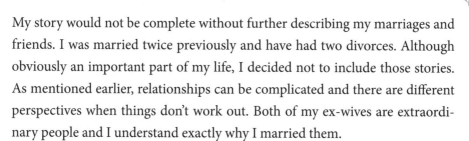

My story would not be complete without further describing my marriages and friends. I was married twice previously and have had two divorces. Although obviously an important part of my life, I decided not to include those stories. As mentioned earlier, relationships can be complicated and there are different perspectives when things don't work out. Both of my ex-wives are extraordinary people and I understand exactly why I married them.

With Wendy, I have two wonderful children, Yoshio and Presley. I could never regret our relationship because of them. The days of their birth were both the best of my life. Suzanne is someone for whom I have great respect and admiration. Like me, she is biracial with a Black father and Japanese mother. Kinobu, her mother, was like a mother to me. I regret that she had to witness our marriage end before she died. It broke her heart.

It took three tries, but I now know that I am in a committed, lifelong relationship with Jacqueline. I didn't always feel that way. Early in our relationship, I lived near the NIH in Rockville, and we took a drive to Ocean City, Maryland. Jacqueline likes telling stories and playing games to pass the time. During the drive, she asked me to pick a movie that I thought best described our relationship. I don't really enjoy playing games and am not much of a storyteller. Somewhat exasperated, I responded, *Mission Impossible*. Wrong answer!

Jacqueline took care of me as I battled prostate cancer, when—for perhaps the first time in my life—I felt vulnerable and needed someone. Through her,

I learned that it was okay to expose my vulnerabilities. She has continued to take care of me, and I delight in taking care of her. After all, even in the *Mission Impossible* movies, the endings—however unlikely at first—are great as the missions are accomplished. The GIs in Misawa often bantered wistfully about their "soul mates." Finding mine has been difficult, but I've finally succeeded.

I have the best friends in the world. I mentioned a few of them in telling aspects of my story, but not all. I cannot adequately describe the depths of my friendships and how special my friends are as people. We don't necessarily spend a lot of time together. We don't even stay in constant contact with each other. However, we love each other and we all know it. It's unspoken, but we all know that we have each other's back. And when we do get together—as infrequent as that may be—it's as if we've never been apart. I didn't mention them all, but they know who they are. And to all of them—thank you!

I wonder, and perhaps even worry, about how Yoshio and Presley will react to this book. They know bits and pieces about my life but not much. One of my motivations throughout life has been to make sure that they do not have to experience the things I did growing up. I couldn't shield them from everything, especially with my divorce from their mother, and they've had their share of life's struggles as well. But they've grown up to be intelligent, caring adults. I love them and am proud of them, more than they will ever know. Both are uniquely gifted. Mom would have been proud of them too.

Both grew up knowing many of my professional ophthalmology friends. After the divorce with their mother, I took one or the other, and sometimes both, to almost every professional meeting I had no matter where it was located. Both became global travelers at a very young age. I marveled at their ease and comfort in interacting with accomplished professionals. They were far more advanced socially than was I at their ages.

I had not intended to write a memoir of my life until after I had retired as university president. Much of what I've revealed is not flattering, and I feared being judged harshly for my and my family's human frailties. I had reasoned that it would be best if I waited until my career would be less impacted by what others thought about me. However, because of the Covid-19 social restrictions, many of my evenings and weekends were suddenly uncommitted. For the first time in decades, I had time to write and I decided to take advantage of it. I understand that some may judge me harshly, but I no longer care. If my story can help anyone, especially young people as they go through their own challenges, that is what is important to me.

I tried to be balanced in my portrayal of my parents. They both made mistakes in their lives, but they evolved with time and were endearing to many.

I wish to acknowledge and thank my sister, Dianna. In writing the book, we had multiple discussions that helped me better remember certain situations. Most of our recollections were very consistent with each other's, but in a few instances, we interpreted certain situations through different lenses. Hearing her perspectives has helped me develop a greater depth of understanding of these situations and has provided me additional insights.

I shared an early draft of the book with Dianna to solicit input and to obtain permission to include sensitive personal information about her. Dianna had some useful suggestions related to my portrayal of others that I tried to incorporate, but she had no suggestions related to herself. I don't know for sure how she really felt but she repeatedly approved what I wrote about her. I appreciate Dianna's willingness to let me share parts of her story. Our early lives were intertwined, and it would have been difficult to tell my story without including parts of hers. We both had a difficult time raising ourselves, but I have a better appreciation now of the struggles Dianna faced that I didn't.

As of this writing, Dianna has been free of gambling for over two years. It helped that access to gambling was initially limited because of the Covid-19 pandemic. More importantly though, her husband, Bob, was diagnosed with a life-threatening leukemia and needed her assistance. She had to decide between his life and her compulsion. She chose his life and I wish them both the very best.

As someone deeply vested in Detroit, one of the slogans I've come to embrace is "Detroit vs. Everyone." It reminds me of what it felt like growing up: "Dianna and me vs. Everyone." As we emerged from childhood, our paths diverged but, like Detroit, grit and perseverance inform our personas. Maybe someday Dianna will write her own extraordinary story.

I will likely never actually retire. Every job I've had—training residents and fellows, taking care of patients, educating college students, performing research, mentoring younger faculty, influencing national policy, interacting with my glaucoma colleagues globally—I've loved. My days as a university president are soon coming to an end, but I will continue to engage in many of these activities with enthusiasm and will feel as privileged as I've always felt to do so. I am thankful to my many colleagues and friends—only some of whom are mentioned in this book—who have provided active support in advancing my career. I am so fortunate to have had them as part of my life journey.

I am profoundly inspired by students, trainees, and young faculty who overcome many barriers and challenges—some greater than my own—in pursuing their goals. I hope that my story inspires them as much as their stories have inspired me.

Finally, life is transitory. My own experience believing I had limited time to live has made me appreciate how precious it is. I consequently try to make the most of each day. Especially important, and something I'm working on, is to make sure that the people I love know that I love them. Growing up, I never once heard my parents say "I love you" to me. I deeply regret that I never once told them "I love you" either before it was too late. It's a mistake I wish not to repeat.

Acknowledgments

I would like to thank the many people who shepherded this book to publication. Elizabeth Atkins, co-creator of Two Sisters Writing and Publishing, Michael Wright, chief of staff at Wayne State, and Annie Martin of Wayne State University Press read an early draft of the manuscript and provided me with much-needed encouragement. Stephanie Williams, the director of Wayne State University Press, also read an early draft. In addition to her helpful comments on the manuscript, she educated this naive first-time author on the publication process and guided me through it.

Ronit Wagman provided expert guidance in further developing this memoir. As each story unfolded, she challenged me to dig deeper and to express the impact of each on my subsequent life. It was not always comfortable for me to do so, but I appreciate the way Ronit exhorted me to explore and express underlying thoughts and feelings. This memoir is richer as a result of her efforts.

My sister, Dianna, was incredibly helpful. Her memories of our time together in Japan were clear and poignant. Much of my story is also her story, and she generously allowed hers to be told unfiltered.

Finally, I thank my wife, Jacqueline, for spurring me on to write this memoir and for tolerating me as it became my single-minded focus for many months.